The 10 Core Competencies for Evidence-Based Treatment

TRAUMA, PTSD, Grief & Loss

MIKE DUBI, Ed.D, LMHC, NCC
PATRICK POWELL, Ed.D, LMHC, LPC, NCC
J. ERIC GENTRY, PhD, LMHC

Published by:
PESI Publishing & Media
PESI, Inc
3839 White Ave
Eau Claire, WI 54703

Cover: Amy Rubenzer
Layout: Bookmasters & Amy Rubenzer
Editing: Marietta Whittlesey

ISBN: 9781683730392

PESI
Publishing
& Media
www.pesipublishing.com

Acknowledgments

To my guiding light and best friend, Jeanne – I am lucky to have you in my life.
To Eric, Patrick and Bob – I am honored to be associated with you. Your knowledge is awesome.
To my clients – I am grateful that you allowed me into a part of your lives.
To my students – I have learned much from you.
And, thanks to PESI for the many training opportunities provided to me.

— Mike Dubi

I would like to extend heartfelt gratitude to the wonderful mentors that have provided for me a milieu of professional development in the field of trauma treatment. In order of appearance in my life, these are: Charles (Charlie) Yeargan, PhD; Louis (Lou) Tinnin, MD (and his wife Linda Gantt, PhD); and Charles Figley, PhD. I wish to extend an extra-special thank you to one of the most gifted clinicians with whom I have ever worked— Robert Rhoton, PsyD. Bob is a vice president of IATP and owner of the Arizona Trauma Institute. I am thankful to my friend and partner in this book and all endeavors IATP—Mike Dubi, Ed.D. I would also like to acknowledge Patrick Powell, Ed.D for all his hard work. Additionally, I would like to thank PESI for 10 great years of opportunity to provide this and other trainings to thousands of professionals across the country.

I would like to thank my friends and family for supporting me as I pursued my education and my career. In particular, I'd like to thank my best friend Chelsea for patiently waiting while I worked on my dissertation, manuscripts, and lesson plans. Also, I'd like to thank my mother for instilling in me a desire to learn and continue to become better. And last but not least, I'd like to thank every student I have had who has asked that one question that I didn't know, resulting in me continuing to further my education.

— Patrick Powell

On a personal note, I am also grateful to the rooms and people of 12-Step fellowships for saving my life and helping me to mature into a professional capable of doing this work. I have had for wonderful sponsors in my nearly three decades of recovery and these incredible folks are: Joe M.; Hellen K., Augie G., and Rick O. Thank you for always being there. Marjie Scofield, MSW is my wonderful partner without whose unwavering love and support I would be unable to withstand the rigors of this work. Finally, I wish to thank and honor the thousands of trauma survivors with whom I have had the privilege to walk. I have been gifted more by your courage, strength and indomitability than I have ever given you. Thanks to each of you for believing in yourselves and the miracle of healing. My portion of this book is offered in your honor.

— J. Eric Gentry

A Dedication to Louis Tinnin

— by Eric Gentry

I divorced in 1995 after a short four-year marriage. My ex-wife was a psychiatrist and we had a practice together in Southeastern West Virginia. As our marriage ended, she decided that she was going to stay in the town in which we were living while I was going to find a graduate school where I could complete my doctorate. However, I was in no shape to begin a doctoral program and had no idea what program I wanted to pursue. During this time, I became aware of the work of Louis Tinnin, MD at West Virginia University in Morgantown.

I had already begun to specialize in trauma in the practice I shared with my ex-wife. I had become trained in EMDR, hypnosis, some of the CBT approaches and NLP. My caseload at this time was made up almost entirely of trauma survivors and I was finding, paired with these new approaches I was learning, I also had some innate savant capacities when working with this population. I had already decided that the rest of my career would be dedicated to working with traumatic stress.

As the divorce was finalizing, I learned that Lou had just announced that he was beginning a new six month fellowship in psychotraumatology. While there was no pay associated with this fellowship, the fellows would be granted faculty status at WVU's School of Medicine and would get a hands-on intensive education working with traumatic stress and dissociation. This fellowship was designed to start with the rudimentary skills of assessment and interviewing and help the readers mature into seasoned and highly skilled trauma clinicians utilizing Lou's (and his art therapist/psychologist wife, Linda Gantt, PhD) model of treatment for traumatic stress and dissociation that he called, at the time, Time-Limited Trauma Therapy. I was one of the first to have begun this mentorship program that Lou continued to offer for the next 15 years.

I spent from July 1995 until May 1996 in Morgantown working with Lou and Linda. It was one of the most valuable learning experiences of my life. Lou has been, by far, the most knowledgeable and skilled clinician I have ever observed in working with trauma and dissociation. He was one of the first to have developed a non-abreactive form of trauma treatment and one of the pioneers in looking at trauma more as a memory problem than a psychological disorder. His contributions to the field are numerous and we lost one of our greatest clinicians ever when he died in 2013. His wife, Linda, continues their work at the Institute for Trauma Therapy in Morgantown, WV. They published a book entitled *The Instinctual Trauma Response* (Tinnin, & Gantt, 2013) shortly before Lou died. This book captures most of his salient ideas and treatment strategies. I am deeply grateful that I had the opportunity to work with and beside him as he helped me forge the foundation of my traumas treatment skills.

Table of Contents

Introduction. xi

The Ten Core Competencies xiii

Chapter 1: Accelerated Trauma Treatment: The Active Ingredients Approach. 1

Chapter 2: Tools for Hope: The Perceived Threat, the Autonomic Nervous System, and Self-Regulation. 17

Chapter 3: Posttraumatic Stress: Illness or Injury? The Instinctual Trauma Response 27

Chapter 4: Conceptualizing and Diagnosing using the DSM. 37

Chapter 5: Tri-Phasic Model: Establishing Safety 51

Chapter 6: Tri-Phasic Model: Remembrance and Mourning. 63

Chapter 7: The IATP Narrative Exposure Therapy (NET). 75

Chapter 8: Grief, Loss, and Mourning 81

Chapter 9: The Next Phase for Trauma Treatment 91

References 93

Appendix A: Trauma History: From Hysteria to Evidenced Based Treatment 97

Biography

MIKE DUBI, EDD, LMHC, NCC, is president and co-founder of the International Association of Trauma Professionals and Editor of the *TraumaPro* newsletter. He was an associate professor and taught in the Counselor Education and Supervision, Clinical Mental Health Counseling, Forensic Psychology and Counseling Psychology programs at Argosy University/Sarasota for 17 years. He has been engaged in the practice of individual and group psychotherapy since 1969 and is a Florida Licensed Mental Health Counselor and Qualified Supervisor. His clinical practice currently focuses on traumatic stress, sex offenders and performance enhancement for athletes and musicians. Dr. Dubi is certified in Cognitive-Behavior Therapy, Hypnosis, EMDR and Brainspotting. In addition, he is also a Diplomate and Board Certified Expert in Traumatic Stress, a Certified Expert Trauma Professional, Certified in Acute Traumatic Stress Management, trained in Accelerated Resolution Therapy, Certified in Disaster Mental Health by the American Red Cross, is a Certified Compassion Fatigue Specialist, and is Diplomate and Clinical Mental Health Specialist in Trauma Counseling.

Mike has been involved in the administration of various private agencies and programs in the United States and the United Kingdom for over 40 years. His businesses have provided consultation, program development, program evaluation, and grant writing services for more than 35 years. He is actively involved in research on traumatic stress and sex offenders.

PATRICK POWELL, EDD, LMHC, LPC, NCC, is a practitioner, counselor educator, and a researcher. He has a clinical background providing treatment to children, adults, families, and sex offenders in non-profit and two private practice environments. Dr. Powell has taught mental health counseling and counselor education programs at the University of Tennessee at Chattanooga, Argosy University/Sarasota and Atlanta Campuses, and Webster University.

J. ERIC GENTRY, PHD, LMHC, is an internationally recognized leader in the study and treatment of traumatic stress and compassion fatigue. His doctorate is from Florida State University where he studied with Professor Charles Figley—a pioneer of these two fields. In 1997, he co-developed the Accelerated Recovery Program (ARP) for Compassion Fatigue—the world's only evidence-based treatment protocol for compassion fatigue. In 1998, he introduced the Certified Compassion Fatigue Specialist Training and Compassion Fatigue Prevention & Resiliency Training. These two trainings have demonstrated treatment effectiveness for the symptoms of compassion fatigue and he published these effects in several journals.

Dr. Gentry was original faculty, curriculum designer and associate director of the Traumatology Institute at Florida State University. In 2001, he became the co-director and moved this institute to the University of South Florida where it became the International Traumatology Institute. In 2010, he began the International Association of Trauma Professionals—a training and certification body—for which he is vice-president. He has trained thousands of professionals to more effectively treat traumatic stress. In 2005, Hogrefe and Huber published Trauma Practice: Tools for Stabilization and Recovery—a critically acclaimed text on the treatment of traumatic stress for which Dr. Gentry is a co-author. The third edition of this text was released in 2015. He is the author of numerous chapters, papers, and peer-reviewed journal articles in the areas of traumatic stress and compassion fatigue.

Dr. Gentry is a licensed psychotherapist with over 33 years of clinical practice. He is the CEO and owner of Compassion Unlimited—a private psychotherapy, training, and consulting practice in Sarasota, FL.

Introduction

Trauma, PTSD, Grief & Loss: The 10 Core Competencies for Evidence-Based Treatment is the result of more than 1,000 presentations sponsored by PESI, the International Association of Trauma Professionals (IATP), Arizona Trauma Institute and other organizations. The presentations were delivered to audiences of mental health clinicians around the world. This final work is a compilation and integration of trauma theories and interventions developed by some of the foremost traumatologists in the world.

This book was written for experienced clinicians, students and other professionals who work in the field of trauma. It provides basic knowledge about psychological trauma which can enhance the understanding and practice of trauma therapy.

Each chapter covers the most important aspects of trauma treatment by using the 10 core competencies as a guide and including a variety of exercises and sidebars. We believe that learning these competencies is essential for all professionals who work with psychological trauma. It is hoped that after reading, mental health professionals will have developed a solid understanding of the foundations of trauma therapy.

— Mike Dubi, Patrick Powell, Eric Gentry

The 10 Core Competencies of Trauma, PTSD, Grief & Loss

(1) Utilization of the Evidence-Based "Active Ingredients" for Successful Trauma Treatment and Complicated Grief

(2) Appropriate Use of the Therapeutic Relationship & Positive Expectancy

(3) Evidence-Based Treatments of Posttraumatic Stress

(4) The Role that Perceived Threat and the Autonomic Nervous System Plays in the Development and Continuation of PTSD Symptoms

(5) Causes and Symptoms of Posttraumatic Stress

(6) Appropriate Assessments for Posttraumatic Stress

(7) Achievement of "Good Enough" Safety and Stabilization (Phase I)

(8) Cognitive-Behavioral Method(s) that Desensitize and Reprocess Trauma Memories (Phase II)

(9) Reconnection Phase of Treatment (Phase III)

(10) Resolve the Grief and Other Peripheral Issues Accompanying Treatment of PTSD

CHAPTER 1

Accelerated Trauma Treatment

The Active Ingredients Approach

COMPETENCIES IN THIS CHAPTER

- Utilization of the Evidence-Based "Active Ingredients" for Successful Trauma Treatment and Complicated Grief

- Appropriate Use of the Therapeutic Relationship & Positive Expectancy

- Evidence-Based Treatments of Posttraumatic Stress

POSITIVE EXPECTANCY

Positive Expectancy is the expectation that a positive meaning can be found in every situation (Langens & Schüler, 2007). Another important facet of Positive Expectancy is that every client can "get better." As counselors, we espouse this idea and model it for our clients. While a number of authors have written on the topic, Viktor Frankl, an Austrian neurologist and psychiatrist, is largely credited for the positive expectancy movement. Frankl asserted that an individual could find meaning or hope even in the harshest of situations. To better understand his philosophy, we should explore his history.

Prior to 1942, Frankl practiced in several clinics in Vienna. He had a specific interest in treating clients with depression and suicidal ideation. However, as he was Jewish, he was forbidden to work with Aryan patients during this time in Austria. In 1942, Frankl, his wife, and his parents were deported to a Nazi ghetto where he worked as a general practitioner in a medical clinic. While there, Frankl set up a suicide watch and offered services to help newcomers suffering from shock and grief. In 1944, Frankl and his wife were transported to Auschwitz. By 1945, Frankl had been transferred to three other Nazi camps. During his time in the camps, he was forced to perform medical atrocities on the cadavers of people he had known and went without food, water, and proper clothing. He remained at Turkheim until he was liberated by American forces. Except for his sister who escaped to Australia, all his family died in the camps.

After living three years in concentration camps, Frankl returned to Vienna to practice. In 1959, Frankl wrote *Man's Search for Meaning* (Frankl, 1959). In this work, he espoused that even suffering the harshest conditions, individuals can choose how they respond. Individuals can find meaning even in the worst of situations, and every individual has the capacity for finding joy, peace, meaning, and love.

> *Between stimulus and response there is a space. In that space is our power to choose our response. In our response lies our growth and our freedom.*

> *Everything can be taken from a man but one thing: the last of human freedoms-to choose one's attitude in any given set of circumstances, to choose one's own way.*

Frankl's influence can be found in a number of models of therapy. His works served as the basis for *logotherapy* a model of therapy that is founded upon the belief that striving to find meaning in one's life is the primary, most powerfully motivating and driving force in human beings (Saraswathi, 2013). Irvin Yalom, recognized by some as the father of *existentialism* often credited Frankl as a primary source (Frankl, 1967). Frankl's influence can also be observed in the therapy model *positive psychology* (Peterson, 2009).

Frankl's message is indeed powerful, but how does it relate to treating clients with traumatic reactions or PTSD? Clients with trauma have experienced a terrifying, harsh, or dangerous situation. Many of those individuals may have felt absolute horror or helplessness. They may be unable to see meaning in the traumatic event and feel afraid to discuss it. However, our clients have the possibility of finding hope and meaning in the traumatic situations they experienced. Further, they can be helped to feel empowered by the ability to choose how to respond to the traumatic event. Nothing can undo the traumatic event, but, individuals can choose to respond to it in any number of ways, including limiting the influence of traumatic events, being proactive in seeking treatment, or helping others. For example, an individual who experienced a sexual assault may be able to find meaning in the experience. She may choose to view herself as a survivor instead of a victim. He may find strengths that he was previously unaware of. These patients can be helped to find a new life goal or direction such as advocating for safe sexual or dating practices. They may choose to become a counselor or a therapist to help others who have had similar experiences.

Clients Can Feel Better

In addition to finding the positives in their experience, individuals need to know that they can feel better. Several authors (e.g., Lynch, 2012; Katerelos et al., 2015), both in the medical and mental health fields, have established that clients who believe that they can get better have a higher chance of doing so. So what do we do as counselors to instill hope in our clients? Many of them will come to therapy feeling as though they cannot succeed or get better. As counselors, we need to model hope and the conviction that everyone has the chance to get better and to change.

However, we should not push our clients. Some counselors will push interventions or move forward with therapy at times when the client isn't yet ready. This is often due to our own anxiety about treatment progress or the client's well being. When clients attempt to slow the process or disengage from treatment, some clinicians will label the response as *resistance*. However, it may not be resistance; many times it is good judgment. Our clients can sense when we are anxious or when we make decisions that aren't based upon them. Many of those clients want to be healed, though, so they stay engaged. They may move forward, but remain guarded. As clinicians, we want our clients to minimize their defenses, see a hopeful new future, and pursue that.

Remember we as counselors may not see an immediate impact of treatment for some of our clients. However, if we have helped our clients develop positive expectancy, we have laid the groundwork for future change. We have instilled the idea that a person can change.

It should be noted that many of our clients, due to previous trauma, are reacting to stimuli a majority of the time. If individuals are constantly in the process of reacting to stimuli, they may not have the capacity to think about their thoughts and the situation. When we provide hope, we provide some distance between the stimulus and

POSITIVE EXPECTANCY CHECKLIST

- A positive meaning or value can be found even in the worst of situations.
- Every client should have hope, or optimism, that he or she can "get better." As clinicians, we model that hope for our clients.
- A significant portion of successful outcomes across therapies is the result of positive expectancy.

the response: a place where a person can consider what he or she wants to do based upon thinking instead of reacting.

It is noted in the literature that trauma-focused treatments are up to 86% more effective than no treatment at all or than various supportive therapies (Bison & Andrew, 2005). Just initiating treatment for trauma appears to be an important first step in helping a victim of trauma. Beyond this, there is disagreement among researchers as to whether treatment is more effective using manualized therapies or whether the person of the therapist is the most important component of effective therapy. Some researchers claim that there is little difference in outcome among different therapies. In 2010, a study at the Department of Veterans Affairs ranked treatments by their effectiveness (The Management of Post-Traumatic Stress Working Group, 2010). The researchers explored the entire treatment continuum in an effort to denote best practices for the treatment of individuals with posttraumatic stress disorder (PTSD).

Veteran's Affairs Office Recommendations

- A supportive and collaborative treatment relationship or therapeutic alliance should be developed and maintained with clients with PTSD as early as possible. Also, a feedback system should be developed by counselors, allowing for clients to make recommendations about the therapeutic relationship or treatment.
- Evidence-based psychotherapy and/or evidence-based pharmacotherapy are recommended as first-line treatment options.
- Specialized PTSD psychotherapies may be augmented by additional problem-specific methods/services and pharmacotherapy.
- Counselors should consider referrals for alternative care modalities (acupuncture, yoga, massage, etc.) for symptom relief, consistent with available resources and consonant with patient belief systems.
- Clients with PTSD who are experiencing clinically significant symptoms, including chronic pain, insomnia, and anxiety, should receive symptom-specific management interventions.
- Management of PTSD or related symptoms may be initiated based on a presumptive diagnosis of PTSD. Long-term pharmacotherapy will be coordinated with other interventions.

The researchers also stratified various treatments into five levels. The treatments noted in level A were supported by strong evidence. Treatments in level A are the recommended interventions for PTSD. The treatments in level C are recommended approaches for specific symptoms. Level C treatments can also be utilized in conjunction with level A treatments. Counselors treating clients with complex PTSD (PTSD that results from chronic long-term trauma such as sexual or emotional abuse) would utilize most of the level C treatments. Research supporting the treatments in level I is inconclusive. There isn't enough evidence on treatments in level I to warrant effectiveness. The table is listed on the following page.

Level	Treatments
A Strong evidence + First-line Recommendation	Cognitive behavior therapies (prolonged exposure, direct therapeutic exposure, cognitive processing therapy, and stress inoculation training), and eye movement desensitization and reprocessing (EMDR)
B Good evidence + second line recommendation	No therapy
C Fair evidence + no recommendation	Patient education classes, imagery rehearsal therapy, psychodynamic therapy, hypnosis, relaxation techniques, group therapy, family therapy, and trauma-focused supportive therapy
D Contraindicated	None
I Inconclusive	Web-based cognitive behavioral therapy, dialectical behavioral therapy, acceptance and commitment therapy, along with complementary and alternative medicine approaches such as yoga, acupuncture, mindfulness, massage

Adapted from Management of Post-Traumatic Stress Working Group

The VA study was published in 2010. However, further research has been assimilated. For example, *feedback informed therapy* (FIT), a topic explored later in this chapter, is now considered a level A treatment. It should be infused into any treatment plan so as to maximize the effectiveness of the treatment.

Case Study

The Relationship Between Adult PTSD and Early Trauma

· ·

In 2011, I worked with Thom, a veteran who served 7 tours of combat in Iraq and Afghanistan. He was diagnosed with PTSD and came to see me at the urging of his wife who threatened to leave him if he did not participate in psychotherapy. He agreed to see me but was also prepared to hate me and to hate therapy. As he came into my office and we shook hands he began laughing and said that I looked like his grandfather, the only family member he liked and I thought looking like a grandfather was an interesting psychotherapy technique. He began by talking about his combat experiences and how powerful they were.

But, as I listened, I also thought there was little real evidence to suggest symptoms of intrusion, avoidance, negative alterations or arousal, the main symptom clusters for PTSD. And, although we both got a little teary at some of the events he shared, I was perplexed as to how the original diagnosis was made until he began to talk about his early childhood - especially the relationship with his stepfather.

Thom's biological father disappeared permanently when he was 3 and his mother destroyed pictures and all evidence of his father. She changed his last name to hers. When he was 7 his mother remarried and the new stepfather was a brute to this child. For example, he would frequently slap Thom on his head for no reason. Once, when Thom was sitting and watching TV, the stepfather hit him so hard that Thom actually was lifted from the chair and flew across the room. Whenever Thom had a bad report card (which was most report cards), he was severely punished. This consisted of the stepfather having Thom sit on a chair facing the stepfather who would repeatedly hit him on his head with a spoon until Thom's head began to bleed. While the stepfather was hitting him with the spoon Thom watched the stepfather become sexually aroused. We often describe men like the stepfather as being sexual sadists. These men often marry certain women to get to their children. This sexual abuse continued until Thom was 11 and the stepfather left the family.

There is a great deal of material written about the relationship between child sexual abuse and later PTSD and we spent most of the remaining therapy sessions working on this early abuse. In particular, we used EMDR therapy which was originally developed to help clients reduce the dysregulation produced by traumatic memories. By accessing, bringing up and desensitizing these memories, the dysregulation is relieved. Thom had 14 EMDR sessions before we could terminate treatment.

— Mike Dubi

CHANGING THE PARADIGM

In 2008, Benish and co-workers published a meta-analysis of outcome research related to treatment for PTSD from the 1980s to the time of the publication (Benish, Imel, & Wampold, 2007). The authors reviewed a variety of research articles from multiple journals and ultimately noted that there were no differences in outcomes among psychotherapies. All treatment types resulted in equivalent benefits. Their results suggest that all bona fide psychotherapies produce equivalent benefits for patients with PTSD.

ACTIVE INGREDIENTS

Eric Gentry, one of the authors of this book and a prominent author in the field of trauma, noted four ingredients that result in effective therapy (Gentry, 2002).

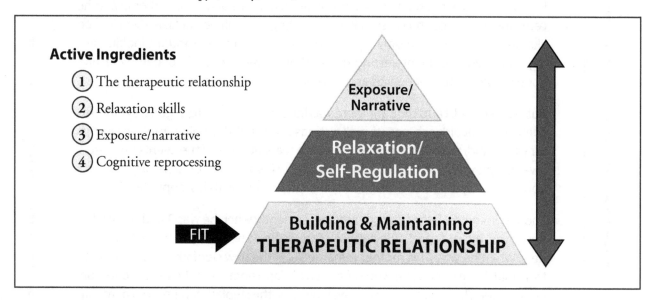

Active Ingredient One:
The Therapeutic Relationship

Typical components of an effective ***therapeutic relationship*** involve developing and maintaining an emotional bond and completing tasks required of one another such as coming to appointments on time and completing agreed upon tasks. Other components of the therapeutic relationship include setting mutual goals and fostering positive expectancy, in other words, finding meaning in the relationship and expecting change. Many authors have noted the importance of the therapeutic relationship. In the previously mentioned report, researchers at the Department of Veterans Affairs noted a supportive and collaborative treatment relationship or therapeutic alliance, should be developed and maintained with patients with PTSD. Additionally, Miller and co-workers remarked that the therapeutic relationship is most often cited as one, if not the most, potent transtheoretical ingredient of psychotherapy (Miller, Hubble, Chow, & Seidel, 2013). Many individuals who have experienced traumatic events have trust and safety issues. Maintaining a safe relationship and environment is critical for the client to progress.

Active Ingredient Two:
Relaxation Skills

The next active ingredient, ***relaxation skills***, includes reciprocal intervention (exposure combined with relaxation). Relaxation is common to all effective treatments for traumatic reactions. Trauma survivors have difficulty regulating their *autonomic nervous systems* (ANS), the system responsible for respiration, cardiac regulation, vasomotor activity, and reflex actions. This lack of regulation can result in increased panic, anxiety, or distress symptoms. However, individuals cannot maintain these PTSD symptoms in a relaxed body.

Teaching our clients to regulate their ANS results in diminished distress and PTSD symptoms. Effective treatments include not only teaching relaxation, but coaching clients toward mastery when monitoring and regulating their ANS. Softening muscles through relaxation while confronting perceived threats is a core component of trauma treatment. Clients must be able to keep their bodies relaxed while confronting traumata, or treatment can cause further trauma for the clients.

In the past, interventions have focused on flooding, or continually reviewing traumatic memories regardless of anxiety level. The idea was that clients would become so aroused that they would enter catharsis, or emotional release, resulting in desensitization. In 1992, Van Der Hart and Brown authored an article titled *Abreaction Reevaluated* (Van Der Hart & Brown, 1992). The authors stated that clients do not need an abreaction, or catharsis, to heal trauma. Trauma is healed when individuals are able to relax their bodies, desensitize themselves, and integrate fragmented memories.

Clinicians should model and practice self-relaxation when intentionally exposing clients to the traumatic situation or memory. Clients will likely feel anxiety, terror, or panic while trying to integrate memory fragments. Remember that thoughts are typically distorted much less frequently when individuals maintain relaxed bodies and are able to utilize their neocortex. This also allows any cognitive distortions that are present to be much more easily confronted.

Active Ingredient Three:
Exposure/Narrative Therapy

The third active ingredient, ***exposure therapy*** (sometimes called narrative therapy) includes sharing a chronology of the traumatic event with the counselor or another safe person. Exposure therapy is also common to all effective treatments for trauma. Exposure therapy is an essential process for the client to integrate traumata that is repressed, suppressed or dissociated. A variety of treatment techniques involve exposure therapy. For example, prolonged exposure, cognitive processing therapy, and EMDR use exposure processes.

In 1954, behaviorist Joseph Wolpe published a paper about his theory of reciprocal inhibition (Wolpe, 1954). He suggested that individuals would not feel anxiety if they maintained a feeling that was incompatible with feeling anxious. At the time, he recommended aggressiveness as an alternate, or incompatible, feeling. As modern counselors treating trauma, we would apply his idea by teaching people relaxation, a condition that is also incongruent with anxiety. When individuals develop a narrative of the stressor or event with a relaxed body, they are able to integrate that traumatic memory instead of reacting to it. For example, a client who has been in an auto accident may find that he has increased anxiety (conditioned response) when riding in a car (conditioned stimulus). The conditioned response (fear, anxiety, panic) cannot occur when a person is relaxed. As clinicians, we must teach our clients to relax when experiencing reminders of the traumatic situation.

Often, a verbal narrative is the most potent form of exposure. Telling a verbal narrative requires the client to think about the event, sequence what occurred, and use language related to the event.

Case Study

The Power Of The Reframe

• •

Phil is a Viet Nam veteran in his early 70's who served two tours and was awarded a purple heart. He was eventually diagnosed with PTSD. Phil first came to see me in 1999 because of a recurring nightmare he experienced several times a week. These began after his discharge in 1973. Phil dreamed that someone entered his bedroom trying to harm him. Phil would awaken suddenly in an agitated state. Sometimes he was so frightened that he reached for the loaded pistol on his nightstand which he would discharge in his bedroom.

In his childhood, Phil experienced extreme anxiety and panic attacks which lasted throughout his life, and nightmares which stopped when he began Junior High School. The panic attacks were so severe that, as a young adult, the first time he had the opportunity to be sexually intimate he had a panic attack and never again allowed himself to have another sexual or romantic experience.

We began working on his nightmare in therapy and nothing seemed to work. Phil visited sleep doctors and took a variety of medications, some of which were experimental, and nothing seemed to work. At some point his nightmares were becoming more frightening - he didn't know if he could survive them. He could not go to bed at night but sat in a chair with his loaded gun. I asked if it was possible that the intruder was not the evil person he thought but was, maybe, someone coming to help him. Phil ran from my office, cursing me because he thought I did not believe he had nightmares. Phil did not respond to my texts, voicemails or a note I left at his home.

I am often amazed at the effectiveness of therapy and, in particular, the power of suggestions. The following week Phil came to my office with an ice cream cake that had SORRY! written on it. It seems that several nights after he left my office he had a nightmare and, in that dream he saw himself, very frightened but confronting the person in his nightmare, and asking why he was there. The person said he had been trying to help Phil for many years but Phil would not allow him. Phil has never had another nightmare. Such is the power of the reframe and the importance of clients creating a meaningful narrative about their traumas.

— Mike Dubi

Active Ingredient Four:
Cognitive Reprocessing

The last ingredient, *cognitive reprocessing*, includes normalizing the client's symptoms, correcting the client's perceptions of his or her safety, and providing psychoeducation. When treating trauma, psychoeducation can help the client process and understand the symptoms of PTSD.

For example, it is of benefit to many clients if the therapist explains that people with PTSD symptoms are not experiencing pathology, but are having normal responses to real events. Their symptoms are from over-adapting to painful experiences in the past. Those previous painful experiences are now intruding upon the perceptual framework of the present, resulting in their developing hypervigilance. Clients may also benefit from being informed that they have already survived the hard part of the experience; all they are doing presently is recovering.

Cognitive restructuring may also include psychoeducation. Clients may benefit from knowing the relationship between the survived event they experienced, perceived threats they have in the present, and their ANS reactions to these threats. The therapist can also explain how PTSD or other traumatic reactions are a way of protecting oneself during the healing process. Additionally, it may be beneficial to explain that memory fragments of the survived event are causing distress in the present because they have not been integrated, and that the key to being able to integrate a fragmented memory is relaxation. Clients may feel more comfortable when it is explained that shame is our way of dissociating from a past history of trauma. An individual should not feel guilt from his or her adaptive behaviors. When clients are able to integrate their narratives, they will then understand why they do certain things that previously made them feel ashamed.

Other psychoeducation techniques may include educational material, validation and normalization of thoughts and feelings, correction of cognitive distortions (causation/world-view), and mindfulness of the present. Other techniques may also include self-monitoring and evolving self-talk.

Case Study

Positive Expectancy Reprocessing Technique

• •

Several years ago I worked with a 25-year-old woman who had a history of being physically, sexually and emotionally abused. Her abuse began in early childhood and she was victimized by her father, brothers and boyfriends throughout her life. After her brothers stopped abusing her, when she was about 14 years old, they told other boys in the neighborhood that they could have sex with her and she was then abused by these boys as well. She left school after the 8th grade, worked in a convenience store and had never traveled more than 25 miles from where she was born.

In therapy we mainly did EMDR and worked on autonomic regulation, assertiveness and self-esteem. She was a motivated, cooperative and enthusiastic client. We would finish her sessions with the technique outlined below to help improve her self-esteem and feel powerful.

After the first session, she was able to visualize herself in a navy blue business suit, white silk blouse, pearl necklace and earrings, expensive shoes and a briefcase, none of which she owned. She then visualized herself walking down Fifth Ave in New York. Wow!

She was finally asked to make herself feel as powerful and positive as the person she visualized. This was such a positive visualization for her that she began to make some powerful changes in her life. She completed her GED and enrolled in college where she got her degree in early childhood education and became a teacher. The techinique is as follows:

1. As it pertains to what we worked on today, please visualize yourself as positively as possible - (make sure it is you in the visualization).

2. Make the visualization as rich and detailed as possible.

3. After you create the visualization, allow yourself to feel powerful and positive.

4. Allow yourself to increase the feelings of power.

5. Do this as many times a day as possible.

6. Do this every day for as long as it is comfortable for at least 21 to 90 days.

— Mike Dubi

THE THERAPEUTIC RELATIONSHIP

Teaching relaxation or cognitive techniques to a client who does not feel safe or trusting would likely be ineffective. Once the relationship has been built, relaxation skills can be utilized so that clients can relax in the moment when experiencing panic, anxiety, or other traumatic reaction symptoms. Once clients can regulate their emotions or anxiety, they will be able to relate what they have avoided: the traumatic event itself. Narrative therapy is then utilized to assist clients in telling their stories so that fragmented memories can be processed as an event that happened in the client's life, and not as something that diminishes or inhibits the client. Cognitive restructuring techniques are utilized throughout treatment to address cognitive distortions the client experiences that may result in depression, anxiety, or fears of safety.

FEEDBACK INFORMED THERAPY

Scott Miller, a prominent researcher of treatment efficacy, studied the top practitioners in a variety of fields to gain a better understanding of excellence, and then later researched the qualities of effective therapies. Miller eventually developed *feedback informed therapy* (FIT) (Duncan, Miller, Sparks, Claud, Reynolds, Brown, & Johnson, 2003).

Key Components of Feedback Informed Therapy (FIT)

- Clinicians should continually collect empirical data to evaluate the quality of the therapeutic relationship.
- Clinicians should gather honest feedback from clients on methods to improve therapy.
- Clinicians should be willing to change techniques to whatever works best for the client.

Miller developed a *Session Rating Scale* (SRS), and he advocates for the use of this scale after every session. The SRS can be found in his website, http://www.scottdmiller.com/. The key foci of the rating scale are four individual scales denoting the client's thoughts on the therapeutic relationship, the goals and topics of the session, the approach or method used by the therapist, and how the session felt to them overall. Clients are asked after the session to indicate positive or negative performance on all four scales. Ideally, counselors review the rating scale between sessions and use the results to improve their therapies.

Session Rating Scale (SSR) Sample Questions

- Did you feel heard, understood, and respected?
- Did you work on or talk about what you wanted to work on or talk about?
- Was the therapist's approach a good fit for you?
- Was there something missing in the session today?

Regardless of whether one uses the SRS or another client satisfaction survey, counselors should utilize some form of survey to improve themselves. Satisfaction surveys can be found in a variety of formats, including mobile phone or tablet versions. For example, the Therapy Outcome Management System uses both the SRS and another tool developed by Miller, the *Outcome Rating Scale* (ORS).

Some clients may feel awkward about rating counselors in front of them, or knowing that the counselor will read the survey afterwards. To remediate this awkwardness, it is recommended that the counselor explain the purpose of the outcome measure, and then not process the SRS at the end of that session. Instead, the therapist should take the measure from the client, tell the client they will discuss the survey in the next session, and wish the client well. Counselors should start the next session by reviewing the SRS with the client. Though there are no specific numerical points on the scales, counselors should be able to estimate how the client's ratings shift during later applications of the SRS. Reviewing the SRS or another outcome measure in the following session should not require more than 5 minutes. Use of the exercise may also provide a focus to the session. If clients are not willing to utilize the measure, they should not be forced to. If clients are ambivalent, then counselors should recommend utilizing the SRS for a few sessions to evaluate it and let the client decide whether or not to continue use of the survey.

Clients should also have the opportunity to verbally give feedback outside of a satisfaction survey; for example, a client may have thought of something between sessions that would better their therapy process. Clients may also want to comment on facets of therapy that are not represented on the measure. Therapists may have differing amounts of feedback from different clients. Some clients will be open to discussion, and will give an in depth response to the satisfaction survey. Other clients may make one or two word statements. This may occur even though the SRS form appears to have all ratings on the far right side, indicating the best performance possible. To address this situation:

Processing the SRS Feedback with Clients

Counselors can ask in a questioning tone, "So it looks like we had a great session last week?"

If a client responds by stating, "Yeah, it was ok," or something equally minimal, counselors can further engage the client by picking the scale that appears lowest, and saying "I notice that you rated this category lowest in last week's session. What did I do, or not do, that resulted in your scoring that one a little bit lower?"

It is important to use the "*I*" pronoun so that the client's response is focused on something the counselor can change or affect.

Counselors can then follow up and ask "What can I do differently in today's session to make it more valuable?"

Some clients may respond, "I don't know," after being asked what can be done differently to improve a session.

A suggestion of how to respond to this situation may be to say, "I'm a good therapist, but I'm not a good therapist yet with you. I want to be, but in order for me to be a good therapist for you, you have to teach me. So, would you please be willing to help me? Once again, what happened last week that resulted in your scoring this category a little bit lower, and what can we do this week to make this score a little bit higher?"

If the client responds appropriately, a good follow-up would be, "Thank you. Now would you, at any time today or in the future, please stop me and let me know if I'm doing something that feels odd or unproductive? Just stop me and let me know what I can do in the moment to make this more valuable for you. Thank you." This type of dialog can develop a collaborative relationship with the client.

As time progresses, it is normal for SRS scores to drop. This may occur because the clients are feeling more honest with the therapist after seeing the therapist reactively respond to their concerns and work to make a therapy session better. Eventually though, the ratings will again rise due to the counselor taking the client's responses into account to develop more effective therapy and to build a more therapeutic relationship with him or her.

Developing, Maintaining, And Enhancing The Therapeutic Relationship

If you review the data from almost every meta-analysis ever completed that looks at therapy outcomes and the factors that contribute to positive outcomes, you will consistently find therapeutic relationship topping the list of most potent factors leading to these positive outcomes. Therapeutic relationship is more powerful, as an ingredient for change, than the actual interventions that we do with our clients. Failing to establish a good relationship will diminish the effectiveness of therapy with a trauma survivor. Conversely, developing and maintaining this positive relationship (through methods like FIT) will significantly enhance your outcomes.

Feedback Informed Therapy (FIT)

The disciplined use of FIT is the most effective and efficient process for enhancing treatment outcomes. FIT allows you to hone into your clients' relational style and provide a therapy experience that fits for them. (IATP) strongly endorses FIT as a foundational cornerstone to excellence in trauma treatment. If you would like to learn more about FIT or acquire the materials needed to begin this process, please visit Scott Miller's website at **www.scottdmiller.com**

In addition to FIT, we have discovered some useful tools for enhancing therapeutic relationships with trauma survivors. Some of these include:

Positive Expectancy

Positive expectancy appears in many meta-analytic studies of psychotherapy treatment as the second most powerful ingredient in initiating and facilitating change. The more hope you can infuse into the process of therapy the more likely your client is to experience positive change from treatment. We are the ambassadors of hope with our clients and, especially early in treatment, we need to have and be able to articulate a clear vision for our clients of how they can resolve their symptoms.

Informed Consent

Informed consent is a psychotherapeutic process and not simply a document to be signed. In facilitating the informed consent process with clients, the therapist should take time to discuss things like potential/expected benefits from therapy (remember 80% of the people (Cooper, 2008) seeking therapy get better) along with the possible negative effects (e.g., uncomfortable feelings, heighted anxiety in the beginning, addressing things the client has been avoiding, etc.).

Therapists should clearly outline the limits of confidentiality and the situations where they are compelled to breach confidentiality (i.e., danger to self or others). Fees, payment methods, cancelled appointments and no shows should also all be part of the informed consent process.

Preparation

Explain the process of therapy early in treatment. Explaining to clients what they can expect from treatment, how the sessions run and how you approach transitions. Your theoretical approach to helping people can have a positive and calming effect for clients who are anxious about attending therapy—especially those who are experiencing psychotherapy for the first time.

Managing Proximity & Permission to Approach

Early in therapy it is good to manufacture a gambit that requires you approaching your client in a safe manner. Before approaching your client ask them, "May I approach?" You should ask this anytime you approach a trauma survivor in therapy. Establishing this ritual early in therapy is an excellent way to communicate to your client that (a) you respect their boundaries and personal space; (b) you are a safe person for them; and (c) you get the issues that trauma survivors have with proximity. This never fails to elevate your value to your trauma survivor clients.

Judicious Self-disclosure

We frequently joke when doing presentations, "Clients love when I self-disclose. . .they just don't care very much about my successes." Like it or not, our clients project on to us all the painful experiences they have ever had with anyone in authority. They are frequently guarded, hostile or afraid of us—especially in early treatment. By sharing some of one's foibles, screw-ups and faux pas, you are allowing your clients to see you as human and fallible.

Goal Setting

Therapy works best when goals are clearly articulated and objectives/waypoints toward those goals are identified. This allows the therapist to continually demonstrate to the client that they are working for them and are focused upon their agenda. These goals should be reviewed and evaluated regularly (at least monthly) to determine (a) progress made toward these goals; (b) impediments to progress; and (c) to determine if there is the need to update and/or change focus of treatment towards a different goal.

Judicious Use of Humor

While it may not be the *best* medicine in psychotherapy, it is still a good one. Self-depreciating humor seems to work quite well in helping clients relax around their therapist. If a therapist can demonstrate care, kindness and competency in their ongoing work with their clients *and* laugh at themselves, these therapists usually enjoy a good therapeutic alliance with their clients.

Rogerian Core Characteristics

Empathy, unconditional positive regard, authenticity/congruence are all important in establishing a therapeutic relationship as is the ability of the therapist to communicate these attributes to the client.

Listening

The better the therapist is able to hear and understand and communicate back to the client that they have heard and understand the client, the better the therapeutic relationship becomes.

Discussing Homework

Discussing the homework assigned/agreed upon with the client during previous sessions lends integrity to the therapeutic process. If a client agrees to complete a project and the therapist does not address this early in the subsequent session, the integrity of the process is damaged. Conversely, if the therapist serves as an accountability partner to the client and the client knows that their homework is going to be discussed, clients are much more likely to complete these assignments. Adam Horvath, in his research on the Working Alliance Scale, was able to demonstrate that the completion of therapeutic tasks was a powerful correlate with good therapeutic relationships.

CHAPTER 2

Tools for Hope

· ·

*The Perceived Threat,
The Autonomic Nervous System,
and Self-Regulation*

COMPETENCIES IN THIS CHAPTER

- The Role that Perceived Threat and the Autonomic Nervous System Plays in the Development and Continuation of PTSD Symptoms

Are you 100% safe right now?

Stop and think about this for a moment. Are you completely 100% safe?

Many people, including our clients, will say, "No." If you responded "no," then your *anterior cingulate* may have atrophied. Your anterior cingulate is in the frontal part of the corpus callosum. It is responsible for two major brain processes: monitoring for conflict and learning based upon rewards. Some researchers are utilizing brain scans of the anterior cingulate as an outcome measure for therapies. This is due to the fact that many individuals with high levels of anxiety or depression have been shown to have diminished volume and electrical activity in the anterior cingulate. Some outcome researchers have also shown that volume and electrical activity can increase in clients, regardless of whether treatment was from psychotherapy or medication.

The world as we know it is based completely upon our senses. We experience the world based upon what we can see, hear, smell and feel. The anterior cingulate is partly responsible for how we filter reality. It allows for an individual to process whether they are safe or if there is a threat in the environment based solely on sensory data, such as what he or she can see, hear, and touch. However, the volume of the anterior cingulate will shrink and its electrical activity will diminish when stress hormones cross the blood/brain barrier. With the anterior cingulate diminished in functioning, individuals will stop making decisions based upon sensory information and begin to make decisions based upon previous experiences and learned data. This can result in a perceived threat where in reality there is none.

17

Real vs. Perceived Threat

- Take the next 10 seconds to experience the room that you are in without using your learning history.

- Try to ignore everything that you have already learned about this room. Attempt to ignore your past learning, and instead, try to identify something in your room that may be dangerous. Look around and experience the room with your senses.

- You may find it challenging to find something dangerous or something that threatens your physical safety within your room.

- There is likely very little that is actually physically dangerous in your periphery.

- If you are still reading this, you are most likely perfectly safe in this moment, and will continue to be safe.

We perceive threats often, but those perceived threats are typically based upon our learned history and not what we are actually experiencing in the moment. Our learned history, if it contains traumata, can come forward with such intensity and ferocity that it significantly colors our reality to where we cannot see what is real, for example, that we are perfectly safe almost all of the time. Any time we have an experience that reminds us of that past learning, it can, and often will, come forward with this intensity so that our body responds with arousal as if we are in danger.

You may look back across your life and realize that the only place you have ever felt actually safety is in the here and now, in the current moment. Or, learned history and perceived threats may come forward with such intensity that you can't enjoy this moment or be in the sanctuary of safety.

Answer the following question: do we live in the safest time in human history? Think about it for a moment. The answer is yes, we do. In 2007, researchers with the *World Health Organization* (WHO) conducted a study on personal safety in the 21st Century (World Health Organization, 2007). The study explored famine, crime victimization, and national disasters. The authors found that individuals who live in medium or high-income countries are living in the safest time in human history. We are the safest known humans to ever walk this planet.

This may make sense but still feel dissonant to you. Though we have less of a chance of danger than previous humans in history, we are also frequently very fearful, perhaps even the more anxious than others in more dangerous times. How can humans be the safest ever, but feel the most afraid? The answer is this: the media.

Our ancestors may have been in much more danger than we are, but we see atrocities and death constantly-on the internet, news, TV shows, and movies. This repeated viewing can be traumatizing, and we are witnessing violence and traumatic situations at an exponential rate in comparison to our ancestors. Every time that we watch something traumatic by watching it on a TV series, by reading a novel, or by hearing a story from a friend, it incrementally raises our level of traumatic stress. Eventually, we can become traumatized without ever experiencing an event that would be considered traumatic.

As an example, have you ever been attacked in a parking garage? Your response is probably no. But do you find yourself more cautious and aroused than normal when alone in a parking garage? Your response is likely yes. Why do we feel more cautious or afraid? Likely, it is because we have heard a story, watched television, or read news articles about people being attacked in parking garages. We have learned that history, so the next time we go into a parking garage, we perceive a threat because of something said by another person.

What happens inside our bodies when we perceive a threat? Our heart rate increases, our respiratory rate increases, our hypothalamus engages, and our chemistry changes to release hormones. Less blood is carried to our extremities and more is carried to our center mass. Our muscles tighten. The only time that an individual will have chronically tight muscles is when he or she perceives a threat. If our muscles are tight, we perceive a threat.

When relaxed, our neurochemical energy is directed towards the outside of our brain to the *neocortex* and other parts of the prefrontal cortex. When a person perceives a threat, all of their neurochemical energy is diverted to the brain stem, the basal ganglia, and the thalamus. As long as we stay in the perceived threat, the longer our neurochemical energy is shifted away from higher thought in the neocortex and directed to the older "reptilian" part of our brain.

When we lose our executive functions, we become unable to function at our normal level of acuity. When a person remains in the perceived threat, he or she loses the ability to communicate through use of normal language. As human beings, we think by using words. When we can't generate our normal vocabulary, the words that we think are designed to separate us from the perceived threat. As an individual stays in the presence of the perceived threat, vocabulary will become more limited, the words used will become harsher and more critical, and speech patterns will begin to accelerate.

THE SYMPATHETIC AND PARASYMPATHETIC NERVOUS SYSTEMS

The neurological changes described thus far are the products of activation of the *sympathetic nervous system (SNS)* which regulates the body's *flight or fight* system. The goal of the SNS is to maintain homeostasis. It is countered by the *parasympathetic nervous system (PNS)*, which is responsible for sleep, digestion, and other activities that occur when the body is at rest. The two systems work together, but are binary, meaning that when one is active the other is not. When we do not perceive a threat, the parasympathetic nervous system is active and we are happy, comfortable, and satisfied. When a perceived threat is introduced, our sympathetic nervous system takes over and we enter fight or flight mode.

Humans have developed to be in a state of SNS dominance. By design, the sympathetic nervous system is meant to be used in spurts. When we need to fight or run, the sympathetic nervous system will activate, giving us the energy we need for survival. Unfortunately, because we have a capacity for learning, humans often operate under a feeling of chronic perceived threat. As a result, our SNS performs at its maximum all of the time, resulting in increased rates of disease and underactive immune systems. As counselors, we must help our clients to relax their bodies. When we are able to relax our muscles, we experience a return of neocortical functioning. Our language skills, judgment skills, and access to all of our learning return. This occurs in just 10 to 30 seconds after the body relaxes. For most individuals, intentional body relaxation requires specialized training, such as learned relaxation skills, exercise, martial arts, yoga, and other techniques.

When our SNS is dominant, our speed and agility are diminished by 20 to 30%. Likewise, our strength is also diminished by 25 to 35%. However, we are receiving rushes of adrenalin, leaving us with the perception that we are powerful regardless of the fact that our ability to engage or evade is diminished. As human beings, we cannot maintain a continuously engaged SNS. We will eventually reach a maximum point of energy where we must fight or flee, engage or run. Remember, the purpose of flight is not to get away from actual danger, but instead to get away from perceived threats. The goal of fighting is also to neutralize perceived threats. This reaction ideally allows our bodies to re-enter a parasympathetic nervous state.

An individual whose sympathetic nervous system is in gear is focused solely on the perceived threat. This threat is present outside of his or her mind and body, which causes the focus to be external instead of on self-regulation or changing one's approach to the perceived threat. Unfortunately, we cannot rid ourselves of all perceived threats. As a result, we must try to minimize or avoid situations where we become overwhelmed by perceived threats.

To explain further, consider that as our SNS engages and neocortical functioning diminishes, we lose the ability to self regulate and maintain self-control. We find ourselves acting out flight or fight instincts against our will, which can result in performing behaviors that may be against our principles. When we do things that breach our personal integrity or things about which we may be ashamed, our actions are because we are not relaxed. Every breach of personal belief and behavior is due to a flight or fight response. Individuals who can maintain a relaxed body are able to use their full neocortex and, with this, can live with integrity and behave in a way that is aligned with their beliefs and principles.

THE ENGINE OF TRANSFORMATION

In order to lead enjoyable lives, our clients have to stop putting energy into things beyond their control, and instead put focus and attention onto the things that are within their control. A large component of this shift in focus involves teaching clients to relax. Unfortunately, many clients are not able or not willing to stop what they are doing at work or at home to begin the self-relaxation process.

Our clients need to be aware that self-regulation is not a total relaxation of the body, but instead, a level of relaxation that allows for the pursuit of daily life activities. We need to teach our clients methods that they can use to relax their muscles while still being able to continue to engage in normal day-to-day life. The more we can relax, the more we can use our neocortex at its maximum capacity, and the more we can be comfortable and enjoy life in alignment with our principles.

There are a numerous ways to relax the muscles within our bodies, or, on a more basic level of thinking about it, to stop squeezing them. As clinicians, we work with our clients to find the methods that work best for them. In particular, techniques that are focused on relaxing the *pelvic floor muscles* allow for a switch from the SNS to the PNS (see worksheets within). Relaxing the psoas, the anal sphincter, and kegel muscles is a component of this process. When the pelvic floor muscles relax, the vagus nerve, the longest nerve in the human body, is able to relax and become stimulated. As a result, we experience an increase in neocortical functioning. Regardless of what we are doing in the moment, our heart rate will stay constant if we maintain relaxed pelvic floor muscles.

Our clients will benefit from being taught to check in with their bodies frequently during the day. This will allow them to recognize tension in the pelvic floor muscles and to relax those muscles. It requires less than a minute to recognize the tension, release it, and return to activities of the day.

LIVING AN INTENTIONAL, PRINCIPLE-BASED LIFE

After our clients have been taught to self-regulate and relax, they are then capable of living a life that is based more upon their own principles and values. Most individuals have a personal code or a set of principles; however, these are not always made explicit. Are you cognitively aware of your principles and values?

For a moment, think of one principle that you try to apply in every situation. Now think for a moment about times when you have acted in a way that did not meet that principle. If you think about those situations, there is likely a trigger, such as a person, place, or event that occurs before you act outside of your principles. Can you discern the trigger? These triggers are perceived threats that engage our SNS and lead to a flight or fight reaction.

Why, though, are these triggers perceived as threats? Simple: our past experiences and learning are intruding upon the present. We are conducting a learned reaction to a perceived threat when there likely is none. If we can consciously relax our bodies, our neocortex will assess sensory data from the situation and we will be able to discern that there is no actual threat. If we are not able to relax our bodies, the sympathetic nervous system will continue to engage, overriding sensory input, and we will enter into our flight or fight response. This process is further detailed in the next chapter.

Continual self-regulation in the face of stressors allows us to not immediately react to a stressor as a perceived threat. As we become more desensitized to stressors, we become more proactive and intentional in our direction and actions, instead of unwittingly allowing our SNS to control our reactions.

Case Study

STOICISM: It Is Virtuous To Maintain A Will That Is In Accord With Nature

• •

Kristin was a 29-year-old nurse who had been diagnosed with fibromyalgia for two years when she first came into treatment. Fibromyalgia is a fairly common disorder which is characterized by widespread pain and tenderness. She had grown up in an emotionally tumultuous family. Her father was an alcoholic Viet Nam veteran with a diagnosis of PTSD who would regularly abuse her mother. Although her father never physically abused Kristin or her siblings, she remembers always being timid and afraid as a child. She also remembers having a very low pain threshold throughout her life.

The month before her first psychotherapy session, she withdrew $10,000 from her retirement account and used it for transcranial magnetic stimulation (TMS) therapy, a technique mainly used to treat depression and insomnia. She received 20-minute TMS sessions every day for a month but at the end her Fibromyalgia remained unchanged.

The very next week she came into treatment. She wanted help because of the negative effect the fibromyalgia was having on her marriage. In the first session we discussed what we could realistically expect from therapy and what was not realistic. This is often referred to as a stoic approach, a term that comes from the Greek philosophy of Stoicism. We worked on how to deal with pain, how to exist at her very challenging nursing job at the local hospital and how to best deal with her increasingly stressful marriage.

She began exercising and taking pain medication as recommended by her physician. The hospital was cooperative in transferring her to a department that could best accommodate her fibromyalgia. We worked on how to better deal with relationships, including her marriage, but also to prepare for divorce (her husband left in week 6 of therapy) and to establish realistic future goals.

The idea that therapy cannot fix every problem is a concept therapists sometimes have a problem with. The National Association of Cognitive-Behavioral Therapist lists Stoicism as one of the key concepts of CBT. Not to have a stoic approach may be unfair to the client.

— Mike Dubi

Self-Regulation

From Sympathetic to Parasympathetic

Recent brain imaging research has begun to demonstrate that anxiety is a brain killer—the more anxiety a person experiences, the less effectively our brains operate. It is becoming increasing apparent that professional and personal effectiveness requires self-regulation skills. By relaxing the muscles of the pelvic region (i.e., kegels, sphincter, and psoas), we are able to effect profound systemic muscle relaxation.

This relaxation facilitates a shift in the autonomous nervous system from the *sympathetic* system (i.e., fight-or-flight reflex utilized during periods of perceived threat) to the *parasympathetic* system (i.e., relaxation and optimal functioning utilized during periods of safety). By maintaining this pelvic relaxation, we are able to thwart the autonomous nervous system from shifting to sympathetic dominance each time we perceive even the mildest threats (i.e. criticism).

By practicing the release and relaxation of these muscles, we can gradually shift from sympathetic to parasympathetic dominance. The rewards of this transformation include comfort in our bodies, maximal motor and cognitive functioning, ability to tolerate intimacy, self-regulation, internal vs. external locus of control, ability to remain mission/principle driven, increased tolerance, increased effectiveness, and increased health of our body's systems.

What happens when my sympathetic nervous system is dominant?

When you perceive a threat, your body responds to either neutralize or move away from this perceived threat. This is true for all species of living things and is known as the "fight or flight reflex." If we are truly in danger of losing our lives, then this reflex is arguably useful.

However, we are rarely confronted with threats and circumstances that are this dire in our daily lives. Instead, we perceive some mild threat and our sympathetic nervous system activates and we find ourselves trying to either kill or run away from our boss, co-worker, or spouse. This over-active and very sensitive threat identification and early warning system is the cause of all stress.

When our SNS is activated and dominant, we are preparing for battle or flight. Our circulation becomes constricted, heart rate increases, and our muscles become tense and ready to act. Inside our brains, the neocortex becomes less functional while the brain stem, basil ganglia, and thalamus become more active. This is because the perceived need to survive has superseded all other brain functioning.

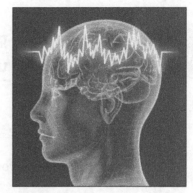

As we become more "stressed" and the longer we are in this state of sympathetic dominance, the more likely we are to compromise the functioning of higher order brain systems such as language, speech, motor activity, filtering, and compassion. This loss of functioning may partially account for why people have trouble thinking logically during "stressful" times, or why they have trouble being kind when they perceive a threat, or even why they have trouble with peak physical performance (e.g., sports) when they are "nervous."

By simply relaxing and keeping relaxed our pelvic muscles we can reverse this process of sympathetic dominance and return to parasympathetic systems. This return to parasympathetic dominance will allow the individual to regain optimal functioning of speech, language (remember intentional thought is simply talking to ourselves—something for which we need to be able to create language and speech), motor coordination, filtering, and compassion.

Once the individual has been able to successfully transition from sympathetic to parasympathetic dominance, without external agents (i.e., drugs) and without regard for the external events then he or she has become self-regulatory. A person who becomes skilled in making this transition has developed an internal locus of control and is no longer a victim of circumstances.

Where are the pelvic muscles?
How do I find them?

While conducting seminars students often ask us this question. We cannot help but feel a twinge of sadness when this question is asked. The sadness comes from the awareness that the person asking this question has learned to be unaware of these muscles. People who are not aware of the muscles in their mid-body are not aware for good reason—it has been a coping strategy since childhood. Children who grew up in anxious and dangerous environments learned to keep their bodies tight in anticipation of danger. With no skills for self-regulating, these children often learn to numb and dissociate their awareness away from the pain in their bodies. They grow into adults who have difficulty being "in" their bodies—difficultly in monitoring and regulating muscle tension and, ultimately, anxiety.

Find And Use
Your Pelvic Muscle

(1)   While sitting, put your hands under your butt.

(2)   Feel the two pointed bones upon which you are sitting.

(3)   Now, touch the two bony points on your right and left side just below the waist.

(4)   You have made a touch memory for four distinct points. Connect those four points to make a square.

(5)   Now, allow your breath to get to the area in the middle of the square. Also, allow the square to expand.

(6)   Release and relax all muscles that traverse the area of the square so that there are NO

       CLENCHED muscles in the square.

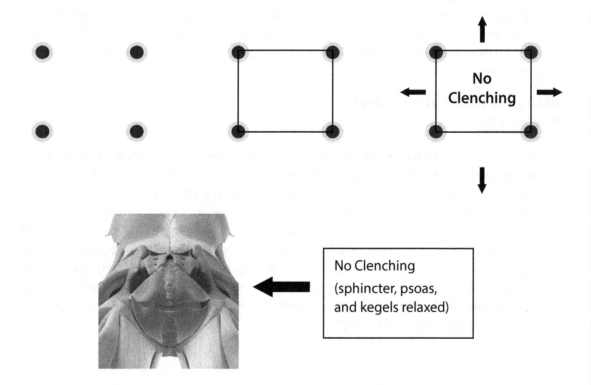

No Clenching

No Clenching
(sphincter, psoas, and kegels relaxed)

What now that my Pelvic Muscles are relaxed?

Simple, keep them that way. If you are able to keep your pelvic muscles released and relaxed for 20 – 30 seconds then you will begin to notice the clear differences in yourself as you transition from sympathetic to parasympathetic dominance. You will first notice comfort in your body. As you release the tension and stress that you yourself have been generating you will become aware that your body is comfortable—no matter what is going on around you. Your thoughts may still be racing and producing warning messages. If this is happening, DO NOTHING; just concentrate on keeping your pelvic muscles relaxed.

This will be difficult for many people because since childhood we have clenched these muscles when we experience this state of alarm. However, if we are able to keep our pelvic muscles relaxed then we will be rewarded with a lessening of "stress" and the restoration of optimal functioning in our thinking and actions. With this self-regulation, we will be able to comfortably seek creative solutions to problems and situations that used to leave us baffled, exhausted, and frustrated.

By developing and practicing the skills of self-regulation we will find ourselves able to maintain fidelity to our intention—our mission. We will find that we no longer need to react to every little crisis as though it is a life-or-death situation. We will become free from our pasts to live for ourselves the lives that we create without having to be perpetually "on guard" for the next danger. We will be able to function at peak effectiveness anytime we choose—a transformation indeed.

Sympathetic = Reactive = Stress = Diminished Functioning = No Choice

Parasympathetic = Intentional = Comfort = Optimal Functioning = Choice

CHAPTER 3

Posttraumatic Stress

· ·

Illness or Injury?
The Instinctual Trauma
Response

COMPETENCIES IN THIS CHAPTER

- Causes and Symptoms of Posttraumatic Stress

Posttraumatic stress disorder (PTSD) is a diagnostic term for a specific combination of symptoms. But how does a person develop PTSD? Some 90% of individuals in the United States have had an experience that could result in PTSD. However, only 10% of those individuals develop the symptoms of PTSD. This is a startling statistic, but it should also illustrate to the reader that not every individual who experiences a potentially traumatic event develops PTSD. So what differentiates an individual who will develop PTSD and an individual who does not? The answer appears to be a sequence of events that occurs within people who are traumatized.

Students in counseling courses often list combat, domestic violence, abuse, national disasters, or sexual assault as traumatic events. However, is there such a thing as a traumatic event? When we assume that an event is traumatic, we assume and sometimes label survivors as traumatized. Sometimes, interacting with people as though they are traumatized has been demonstrated to iatrogenically create symptoms of traumatic stress. So instead of talking to our clients about traumatic events, we instead should talk to them about their experiences to determine whether they had a traumatic response. We may find that they have been able to integrate their experiences without developing PTSD or requiring significant treatment. This approach has been found to maximize recovery and resilience. Remember, there is no one event that always produces PTSD in survivors.

Case Study

A Clinician Overcoming Trauma

. . . .

Maurice was born in Haiti and when he was 7 years old he witnessed his father being assassinated. Maurice was playing in the backyard of his home when he heard noise and hid behind some bushes. He saw his father, hooded and with hands tied, being led into the yard by two men. They pushed his father to the ground and shot him in the head. Maurice was so terrified that he remained frozen for a long time (he is not sure how long) before he was able to find his mother. He began to stutter as he tried to tell the story which caused his mother to become impatient. This created a lifelong stuttering problem which he could control unless he was under stress.

When he was 9 years old, the family moved to the US. Maurice was one of four brothers, a sister, his mother and grandmother. He could not speak English and was placed in a school for children with special needs. He was tested and given a diagnosis of severe mental retardation. He was also constantly bullied by other children.

By the time Maurice was 11 years old he could speak English and was placed in a mainstream school. He graduated from high school as the class valedictorian and eventually earned a Ph.D. in Clinical Psychology specializing in the treatment of PTSD. However, his early diagnosis still remains.

Maurice is frequently traumatized while doing therapy and sometimes experiences panic-like symptoms during or after these sessions. He believes he is able to hide most of his responses from clients and refuses to engage in psychotherapy.

— Mike Dubi

Case Study

Implicit Memories

• •

At age 18 Kevin was a driver at the head of a convoy in Afghanistan. He was in the front seat of the vehicle and his two best friends were sitting behind him. He noticed that the two-lane road he was driving on was beginning to narrow about a quarter mile ahead and remembers thinking that he had better be extra alert. The next thing Kevin remembers was that he was outside the vehicle, which was engulfed in flames and burning, he was deaf and confused and he remembers carrying the helmet of one of his friends and putting body parts of his two friends into the helmet. Kevin had no serious physical injury but his friends were blown to bits. Kevin received a diagnosis of PTSD, was discharged and received a generous disability payment.

When I met Kevin he was 25 years old, with a 13-month-old son and a wife who was 7 months pregnant with their second son. Several weeks earlier the family had gone to the local mall for breakfast. As they were walking towards the food court there was a loud noise – perhaps a falling tray – and Kevin dove under a table where 4 strangers sat. One of the people at the table phoned 911 while Kevin was curled into a fetal position, shivering, muttering to himself and unresponsive to his wife who was frantic. Their child was crying. First responders arrived in record time – about 8 minutes – at about the same time Kevin opened his eyes and asked "what happened?" After undergoing some tests at the local hospital Kevin went home.

Kevin had made the master closet at home into a man cave and he retreated to his man cave as soon as he got home. His wife said he remained there for 9 days. She would bring him food and he would leave empty trays outside the door. His wife said "I know he must have left the room at some point. After all, he must have gone to the bathroom but I did not see him outside the room once." After the 9th day his wife said to Kevin that if he did not go into therapy she would leave him. Kevin agreed to participate in therapy but only if his wife could attend and only if I allowed her to speak for him until he felt comfortable. I agreed to both requests and after the third session Kevin said he felt comfortable enough to do therapy on his own. Kevin was 26 years old at that point. The therapy focused on the implicit memories that made him so fearful of them being triggered again.

— Mike Dubi

OUR BRAINS

Our brains have two halves that serve separate functions. By age 5, our *corpus callosum*, which connects the two spheres of the brain, is fully formed. We are left with a complex and integrated organ that functions as a whole. Our brains work best when in equilibrium, or balance. When our brains are out of balance, such as when information or experiences are encoded outside of consciousness and are suppressed, repressed, or dissociated into the unconscious, our brains will continue to attempt to bring that material into our conscious thoughts.

Human beings have two types of memory. The first type is a *narrative memory*, which is encoded primarily in the hippocampus. The narrative memory is also called the *declarative memory*. It is often associated with language resulting in all of our experiences being sequentially encoded with language as one long narrative. These memories are immediately retrievable.

Paired with our narrative memory, we also have an *implicit memory* that is encoded primarily through the *amygdala*. These memories are primarily sensations such as smells, sounds, and physical sensations that are associated with past events. When recalling events encoded by the amygdala, we experience the sensation associated with each memory.

For example, do you remember your first time riding a bike? If so, your narrative memory is likely being used to recall the specific memory of riding a bike. Your implicit memory may also be in effect, resulting in your recalling a smell in the air or the feel of the wind against your skin. Combined, the two form a total memory of the event.

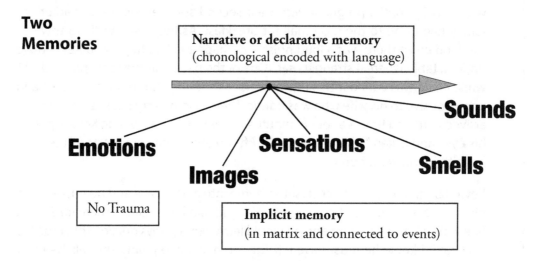

The first animals could not innovate when they felt threatened. When attacked, those animals could only freeze, or stop motion. Eventually, over millions of years, a bulb, the basal ganglia, developed at the end of the spinal column. As the thalamus and other structures developed, we began to innovate. Animals could charge their bodies with energy when attacked. This energy allowed the animal to fight or to flee the perceived threat. This new chance for survival allowed for animals to live long enough to proliferate on a larger scale.

Over time, the limbic system developed with the mammalian brain, allowing for creatures to learn and develop procedural memory. For the first time, creatures were able to develop ways to get what they wanted and ways to avoid things they didn't want. If they completed actions often, those memories would be stored as a sequential process that didn't require thought.

Over time, the neocortex developed. This new component of the brain allowed for higher level thinking, and differentiating between perceived and real threats. We also developed abstract thought and language, allowing us to find further rewards and avoid further threats.

Quadrune Brain Organization
Tinnin & Gantt, 2013

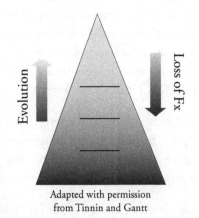

Human - Prefrontal cortex/Broca's/Werneke's

Neomamalian-Limbic

Paleomamalian-Basal Ganglia/Thalamic

Reptilian -Brain stem

Evolution

Loss of Fx

Adapted with permission from Tinnin and Gantt

Threat Avoidance & Evasion (conscious)

Non-Verbal Thought (learned responses/classical & operant conditioning)

Fight or Flight

Freeze

THE INSTINCTUAL TRAUMA RESPONSE

Humans have the ability to limit the use of important areas of our brains. When an individual becomes too scared too quickly, or stays scared for too long, they experience diminished functioning of the prefrontal cortex and the temporal lobe, resulting in the loss of language, thinking, and the ability to relate to others. Developed skills are lost. When executive function is lost, information is available only through the limbic system or through muscle memory. This is one reason why law enforcement and military train frequently: to retain muscle memory. Can you remember a time when you were scared and unable to think? If an individual continues to stay scared, access to the limbic system and will be lost, leaving the flight or fight response.

A variety of factors determine whether someone will choose flight or fight, but the response is rarely predictable. If the fear state continues without action, then freezing or stopping in the face of a perceived threat is the only response left. The mental point of freezing is the origin point for trauma. Trauma occurs as a sequential process beginning with a startle.

Startle

A startle is a perceived threat that has enough energy to overwhelm the nervous system's ability to perceive a threat. Most people who are startled engage in an activity, such as avoidance or attack. Individuals who are able to express their energy by running away, engaging, or talking rarely develop traumatic reactions.

Thwarted Intention

Trauma occurs when flight or fight is thwarted. This can occur in several ways. There may be environmental limitations that prevent fighting or fleeing. An example would be someone trapped in a plane that is about to crash. The environment has prevented them from negating that energy.

Freeze

If an individual is unable to leave the situation or negate the energy, he or she will freeze or stop moving. The person is likely panicking due to the feeling that he or she needs to do something to be saved, but is unable to do anything. Freezing can lead to the development of a traumatic response due to the body memory and the altered state.

Altered States

When an individual perceives a threat, feels unable to negate increasing amounts of energy, and freezes, he or she may enter into a dissociative state. The thwarted energy has reached such a peak that self-management becomes impossible. Consciousness is diminished. Self-identity is no longer present. A person who is dissociating may not know who they are or anything about themselves. Clients may not be able to remember their actions when they are trying to remember the time in altered states. Individuals who enter altered states are likely to develop PTSD. Does a client report an alteration of consciousness during trauma, for instance that time is standing still or that he is outside of his body? If yes, PTSD is likely to develop.

Limiting consciousness requires an enormous amount of energy. This high level of energy directly injures the brain. The traumatic brain injury may not be percussive or concussive, but electrochemical. The way the brain fires neurons is changed. Though our brains can change and become as effective, if not more, than prior to trauma, the neuron firing sequence within the brain for task completion is changed forever.

When we finally lose control of the high levels of energy, we can enter altered states and brain injury can occur. This shuts down frontal lobe and hippocampal function, which inhibits narrative memory of the traumatic event. When this occurs, we can only code memory implicitly. The memories are paired with terror and horror. Even though individuals can only encode implicit memories, these memories are there and can later be recalled and integrated if a person is sufficiently relaxed.

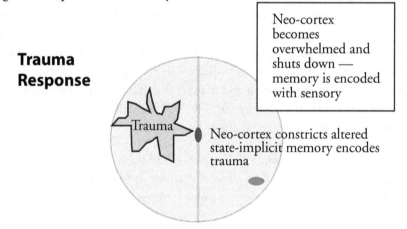

Trauma Response

Neo-cortex becomes overwhelmed and shuts down — memory is encoded with sensory

Neo-cortex constricts altered state-implicit memory encodes trauma

Body Memory: Automatic Obedience

It is worth noting that some individuals in altered states are highly suggestible and obedient. This occurs more frequently with individuals who have had multiple traumas, and more specifically, childhood traumas. Those individuals are also more likely to enter altered states more easily when confronted with perceived threats. These individuals are malleable and easy to manipulate because the frontal lobe capacity and executive functioning that allow for self-control are lost during the altered state.

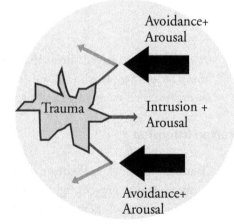

Avoidance+ Arousal

Intrusion + Arousal

Avoidance+ Arousal

Trauma

Resolution

After the event, our clients often speak of sensory memories related to the event. Individuals reporting intrusion symptoms will often report a sight, a sound, or a feeling that suddenly impacts them. As counselors, we serve our clients well by educating them that these flashbacks, nightmares, and other intrusive symptoms are signs of the brain's self-healing system at work. These symptoms are our bodies trying to integrate the memories and the experience. It is an attempt of the implicit memory to bring this fragmented memory into consciousness, give it words, and develop a narrative memory. Our conscious narrative memory avoids or fights this fragmented implicit memory because consciousness was limited or stopped the last time this material was experienced.

Again, prior to trauma, individuals are integrated beings. After experiencing trauma, people essentially become two factions warring over whether to accept or deny the traumatic material. The brain has become polarized. The more an individual experiences traumata, the more polarized he or she may become, resulting in frequent dissociation.

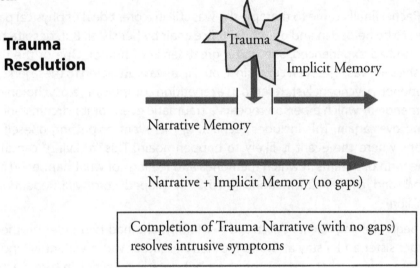

To assist clients in avoiding the fragmented memory, counselors must teach clients to get their bodies relaxed enough so that they lose their compulsive procedural memory. This allows them to use their neocortex to ascribe language to the memory and heal the trauma. As we turn fragmented memories into narratives, trauma becomes healed. Once the individual is relaxed and fragmented memories are integrated, this should cause the client to no longer experience flashbacks or other intrusion symptoms. The client is no longer meeting some of the significant diagnostic criteria for PTSD. The symptoms of PTSD are pathological; they are symptoms of adaptation and self-healing.

Case Study

Vicarious Trauma

• •

Rachel was a 38-year-old woman who had been married and divorced 5 times. Each husband was a violent alcoholic who was physically abusive to Rachel. Husband number 5, the man she loved most and who she wanted to spend the rest of her life with was, by far, the most violent. The morning after their wedding, after being asked by Rachel what he would like for breakfast, he beat her so severely that she was in a coma for almost a week. She had nightmares of the beating which lasted for 6 months and which eventually brought her into therapy.

When Rachel finally came to therapy, she was still in a great deal of physical pain and had to be helped in and out of my office chair by her sister. But, despite the abuse she had experienced, she had a great sense of humor. One of the first things she said was, "I just can't explain it, but I'm always attracted to these jerks," a phenomenon psychoanalysts refer to as a repetition compulsion, a psychological phenomenon in which a person repeats a traumatic event or its circumstances over and over again. This includes reenacting the event or putting oneself in situations where the event is likely to happen again. This "re-living" can also take the form of dreams in which memories and feelings of what happened are repeated, and even hallucinations (https://en.wikipedia.org/wiki/Repetition_compulsion)

As we began talking Rachel described her family. She had two older brothers, a younger sister and a stay at home mother. Her father was a violent alcoholic who abused her mother and two brothers but doted on Rachel. In turn, Rachel adored her father and somehow, although she knew how abusive he was and how frightened she became when her father was abusive, she was always able to forgive him and came to his defense when people said bad things about him. Her defense of her father alienated Rachel and her brothers. Rachel said that she met men in a local bar. Until it was mentioned in therapy it never occurred to her that there may have been a relationship between where she met men and the type of man she was attracted to. Her first response was "where else can I meet men?" When asked if the men she was attracted to reminded her of her father the first thing she said was "oh no, none of them look like him" although as we began to discuss this topic she began to see that there were many things these men had in common with her father. And each time she was exposed to violence on TV or in reality, she responded with feelings of terror. In addition to helping Rachel make rational decisions about men she wanted to consort, with we also worked on her nightmares using imaginal exposure therapy. Exposure therapy is a powerful modality that has the client imagine the traumatic events – the more the client is exposed to the anxiety provoking stimuli, the less anxiety provoking it becomes.

In one of her last sessions, Rachel decided that she would "turn and run" every time she met a man that she was attracted to – a good idea but probably not very practical.

— Mike Dubi

Reframing Traumatic Stress Symptoms: Psychoeducational Interventions

Motivational

- The hard part of your life is over. You survived! The rest of this is just cleaning it up. Therapy is not difficult compared to what you have already accomplished.

- Healing trauma is simple. . .it sometimes is not easy but it is always simple. You only have to complete two things to resolve your symptoms. These are: (1) learn to get and keep the muscles in your body relaxed and, once you have developed this skill, then (2) tell the stories of your trauma(s) to me while keeping a relaxed body.

- You are in the top 10% of resilient people on this planet. I know that because you are here! You are not dead. You are not in jail. You are not actively drug-addicted.

- The absolute hardest part of recovery from trauma is the stopping of avoidance and trying to run away from it. Look at you sitting here in my office ready to confront one of the most frightening things of your life.

- I promise you that if you will put some work into mastering the skills that I am going to teach you, you will be able to lessen your symptoms to a point of comfort and find a new way to live that is not ruled by fear.

Normalization

- All the symptoms of traumatic stress are evidence of a system that is attempting to heal itself from a wound (trauma). With the fear that you have lived in since the traumas of your past, you have prevented your system from completing your healing. What we are going to do is help you arrest your fear and allow this healing process to finish.

- What would any normal/healthy/rational person with your history likely believe about themselves? Their world? Relationships?

- Anytime a human being has a painful learning experience, the next time they encounter any situation that is in any way similar to the previous learning experience, they perceive threat. And what happens inside of a body that perceives threat?

- With a relaxed body you are stronger, faster and smarter than you are if constantly on guard.

- I would like for you to begin practicing "relaxed vigilance" instead of your instinctual hypervigilance.

- You are a normal person having normal reactions to a traumatic past. You are perfectly adapted to the historical traumas of your life. The problem is you have remained at that level of adaptation that you developed and that was necessary in your past. You no longer need that level of sensitivity and vigilance. You are not sick but you are "over-adapted" for a life where there not as many demands upon you as there were in the past.

CHAPTER 4

Conceptualizing Symptoms and Diagnosing Using the DSM

....

COMPETENCIES IN THIS CHAPTER

- Appropriate Assessments for Posttraumatic Stress

The first version of the *Diagnostic and Statistical Manual of Mental Disorders (DSM)*, published in 1952 (American Psychiatric Association [APA]) provided *gross stress reaction* as a first diagnosis for symptoms now known as those of combat-related PTSD. The criteria in this DSM version presented a transient anxiety reaction that would resolve once soldiers were no longer in combat. The subsequent version, *DSM-II*, was published in 1968 (APA). Gross stress reaction was not included in this revision because the symptoms, and the diagnosis itself, were considered by physicians and researchers to be resolvable by removing troops from the battlefield.

In 1980, the *DSM-III* was published (APA). Between the second and third editions of the manual, an influx of soldiers with combat and trauma reactions returned home from Vietnam, which resulted in the need for a diagnosis for these soldiers. After consultation with the American Psychiatric Association, the diagnosis of *posttraumatic stress disorder* was introduced in the "Anxiety" section. It applied to individuals who were exposed to traumatic situations and who experienced strong emotional experiences afterward related to the event. This diagnosis was notable because it positioned the traumatic stressors affecting the diagnosis as external to the individual, instead of as an emotional response by the individual. Also, this diagnosis differentiated traumatic stressors from the normal stressors of everyday life.

PTSD diagnosis included some minor revisions in the *DSM-III-R*, published in 1987 (APA). More important than these revisions, the authors noted in this *DSM* edition that traumatic reactions were far more common in all cultures than previously thought. Further, the authors noted that individuals in countries with frequent conflict, such as Cambodia, Ethiopia, and Gaza, were much more prone to experience PTSD than those in other countries.

The next iteration of PTSD occurred in the *DSM-IV*, published in 1994 (APA). This edition is notable for its revisions to the PTSD diagnosis for several reasons. First, the authors classified symptoms into three clusters: intrusive recollections, avoidant/numbing symptoms, and hyper-arousal symptoms. Next, the authors also included duration of PTSD symptoms and requirements that the symptoms must cause significant distress or functional impairment. Also, for the first time, children were included as individuals who may receive the diagnosis.

The *DSM-5* was published in 2013 and included further changes to the diagnostic criteria (APA). Foremost, the authors recognized that PTSD and other trauma-related diagnoses were so significant that they required their own section. A new section, titled *Trauma and Stressor Related Disorders*, contained a variety of disorders that previously were not conceptualized as being related to PTSD. For example, PTSD is now in the same section as adjustment disorder, a diagnosis of short-term reactions to a stressor or trauma. Also notable, anhedonic/dysphoric symptom presentation was expanded due to many individuals' reporting negative mood states and disruptive behavioral symptoms along with anxiety. In earlier versions of the *DSM*, individuals were required to directly experience a horrific event. However, the new criteria allow for an individual to vicariously experience the situation through watching or reading about traumatic events in the media, hearing about traumatic incidents by word, or even treating clients who tell repeated traumatic stories. New criteria in the *DSM-5* also indicate that the symptoms experienced by the individual must have had their onset, or become exacerbated, after exposure to a traumatic event. The following eight criteria represent the *DSM-5* diagnosis of PTSD.

Criterion A:
Prior Exposure to a Potentially Traumatic Situation

The focus of *Criterion A* is exposure to a traumatic event. The *DSM-5* describes this as *Exposure to actual or threatened death, serious injury, or sexual violence* as evidenced by one (or more) of the following: (1) directly experiencing the traumatic event(s), (2) witnessing, in person, the event(s) as it occurred to others, (3) learning that the traumatic event(s) occurred to a close family member or close friend. Readers should pay close attention to the last sentence. The event had to have occurred to someone that the client is close to. In cases of actual death, the events must have been accidental or violent. (4) Individuals may also meet Criterion A by experiencing repeated or extreme exposure to aversive details of the traumatic event(s) (e.g., first responders collecting human remains; police officers repeatedly exposed to the details of child abuse). You will notice that the fourth method involves an individual's experiencing the event due to his or her professional responsibilities. Individuals who voluntarily seek out potentially traumatic events or images would not meet Criterion A.

It should be noted that this Criterion changed between the *DSM-IV* and *DSM-5*. In the *DSM-IV*, individuals had to directly experience the traumatic event. With the *DSM-5*, individuals can experience the traumatic event second-hand by hearing about it or by providing aid or service to the survivors or handling resulting material evidence. This allows for more individuals, including counselors and crisis responders, to be diagnosed with PTSD.

Criterion B:
Intrusive Thoughts

Intrusive thoughts, the focus of *Criterion B*, often occur after individuals have experienced a traumatic event. In the *DSM-IV*, this grouping of symptoms was titled *Re-experiencing*. To meet this criterion, individuals must experience one (or more) of the following intrusion symptoms associated with the traumatic event(s), beginning after the event(s) occurred: (1) recurrent, involuntary, and intrusive distressing memories of the traumatic event(s), (2) recurrent distressing dreams in which the content and/or affect of the dream are related to the traumatic event, (3) dissociative reactions (e.g., flashbacks) in which the individual feels or acts as if the event(s) were recurring. Such reactions may occur on a continuum, with the most extreme expression being a complete loss of awareness of present surroundings. (4) Individuals may also experience intense or prolonged psychological distress at exposure to internal or external cues that symbolize or resemble an aspect of the traumatic event(s), or (5) marked physiological reaction to external or internal cues that symbolize or resemble an aspect of the traumatic event. It should be noted that the authors included intrusion criteria for children. The most significant aspect of Criterion B for children is that they may display intrusion as reenactment in play and in dreams. As noted in the previous chapter, the intrusion symptoms in Criterion B can be conceptualized as impaired implicit memories of the traumatic event attempting to become a narrative memory.

Criterion C:
Avoidance of Stimuli

Many individuals who have experienced trauma either avoid the traumatic situation, if it is ongoing, or attempt to avoid thoughts and feelings associated with the trauma. In the *DSM-IV*, this criterion was titled *Avoidance and Numbing*, and included seven symptoms. In the newest edition, the authors separated the two parts of the criterion into C and D, and placed the symptoms associated with *avoidance* in Criterion C and *numbing* in Criterion D. *Criterion C* includes persistent *avoidance of stimuli* associated with the traumatic event(s), beginning after the traumatic event(s) occurred, as evidenced by one or both of the following: (1) avoidance of, or efforts to avoid, distressing memories, thoughts, or feelings about, or closely associated with, the traumatic event(s), or (2) avoidance of, or efforts to avoid, external reminders (people, places, conversations, activities, objects, situations) that arouse distressing memories, thoughts, or feelings about, or closely associated with, the traumatic event(s). A common concern with the criterion is that there are only two options, potentially resulting in under diagnosis. Individuals with PTSD will often avoid the traumatic situation because of heightened degrees of arousal and anxiety (Criterion E).

Criterion D:
Negative Alteration in Cognition and Mood

Some individuals develop illogical negative cognitions about themselves, others, or the world, resulting in depressed mood states. *Criterion D* includes *negative alterations in cognitions and mood* associated with the traumatic event(s), beginning or worsening after the event(s) occurred. These must occur as evidenced by two or more of the following: (1) inability to remember an important aspect of the traumatic event(s) (typically due to dissociative amnesia and not to other factors such as head injury, alcohol or drugs), (2) persistent and exaggerated negative beliefs or expectations about oneself, others, or the world (e.g., "I am bad," "No one can be trusted," "The world is completely dangerous," "My whole nervous system is permanently ruined"), (3) persistent, distorted cognitions about the cause or consequences of the traumatic event(s) that leads the individual to blame himself/ herself or others, (4) persistent negative emotional state (e.g., fear, horror, anger, guilt, or shame), (5) marked diminished interest or participation in significant activities, (6) feelings of detachment or estrangement from others, (7) persistent inability to experience positive emotions (e.g., happiness, satisfaction, or loving feelings). It should be noted that Criterion D is an entirely new category; however, options 1, 4, 5, 6, and 7 were previously represented in some form in Criterion C in the *DSM-IV*.

The symptoms in Criterion D, illogical *negative cognitions*, are consequences of the loss of neocortical functioning. Because individuals constantly perceive a dangerous world, they experience decreased executive functioning paired with impulsivity and energy. They have lost the ability to make sense of the world and to change their negative perceptions.

Criterion E:
Alterations in Arousal and Reactivity

Some individuals who experience a traumatic event will find that they experience heightened awareness and reactivity. *Criterion E* includes *marked alterations in arousal and reactivity* associated with the traumatic event(s), beginning or worsening after the traumatic event(s) occurred, as evidenced by two or more of the following: (1) irritable behavior and angry outbursts (with little or no provocation) typically expressed as verbal or physical aggression toward people or objects, (2) reckless or self-destructive behavior, (3) hyper vigilance, (4) exaggerated startle response, (5) problems with concentration, and (6) sleep disturbance (e.g. problems falling or staying asleep or having restless sleep). In the *DSM-IV*, this cluster was titled *Hyperarousal*. It should be noted that option 2, reckless and self-destructive behavior, was not included in previous versions of the DSM.

Those who experience trauma often associate situations, places, and other people with traumatic memories. As a result, individuals often maintain a higher level of arousal and perceive the world as a much more dangerous place than it actually is. Their autonomic nervous system is much more deregulated, resulting in dominance by the sympathetic nervous system, resulting in issues with arousal and reactivity.

Criterion F:
Duration

The remainder of the criteria focus on time duration of symptoms and symptom severity. With *Criterion F*, the duration of the disturbance (Criteria B, C, D, and E) *must be more than 1 month*. Otherwise, acute stress disorder is the more likely diagnosis. Regardless of how long after the event an individual begins to show symptoms, even 6 months after, the symptoms of PTSD have to persist for over 1 month before the diagnosis can be made.

Criterion G:
Functional Significance

As with other mental health disorders in the manual, Criterion G denotes that *the disturbance causes clinically significant distress or impairment* in social, occupational, or other important areas of functioning.

Criterion H:
Exclusion

Criterion H states that the disturbance is not *attributable to physiological effects of a substance* (e.g., medication or alcohol) or other medical conditions.

Specifier:
With Dissociative Symptoms

Assuming that an individual meets criteria A through H, there are two specifiers that can be applied to the PTSD diagnosis: dissociation and delayed expression. In order to meet *with dissociative symptoms*, the individual's symptoms must not only meet all the criteria for PTSD, but, in addition, the individual experiences persistent or recurring symptoms in response to the stressor from either of the following: (1) Depersonalization, or persistent or recurrent experiences of feeling detached from, and as if one was an outside observer of, one's mental processes or body (e.g., feeling as though one were in a dream; feeling a sense of unreality of self or body or of time moving slowly), or (2) Derealization, or persistent or recurrent experiences of unreality of surroundings (e.g., the world around the individual is experienced as unreal, dreamlike, distant or distorted).

Specifier:
With Delayed Expression

The other specifier, *delayed expression*, may apply if the full diagnostic criteria are not met until at least 6 months after the event (although the onset and expression of some symptoms may be immediate).

It should be noted that in the *DSM-IV*, individuals were required to meet six out of 17 symptoms to be diagnosed. In the *DSM-5*, individuals have to meet six out of 20 symptoms to be diagnosed with PTSD.

ASSESSMENTS

A variety of tools are utilized to assess and diagnose PTSD using the DSM criteria. Some are reliable and valid; others are not. The Department of Veterans Affairs lists on their website a few assessments that are commonly used and that have been tested for reliability and validity. In the following sections, we will briefly discuss the *Clinician Administered PTSD Scale* (CAPS) (Weathers, Blake, Schnurr, et al., 2013), the *Post Traumatic Checklist* (PCL) (Weathers, Litz, Keane, et al., 2013), the *Trauma Recovery Scale* (TRS) (Gentry, 1998) and *PIDIB* (Raggi, Dubi, & Reynolds, 2008). Before using these or any other assessment, clinicians should review the laws pertaining to clinical assessment and licensure in your state.

The CAPS is a 30-item structured clinical interview. It is used primarily for diagnosing PTSD. The tool is known for having good psychometric properties and inter-rater reliability. It is considered the gold standard for diagnosing PTSD. The measure is administered and scored by a clinician; it is not a self-report measure. Each symptom of PTSD has a qualitative section used to derive a numerical evaluation of the symptom. The clinician will ask the client a qualitative question to determine whether or not the client is experiencing the symptom. The intensity and frequency of the symptom are measured and used to define severity. A symptom can be scored anywhere from 1 to 4. If a client receives a severity score of 2 (indicating moderate severity) or more, that symptom is considered to be present. One of the benefits of this measure is the ability to denote a global intensity level of PTSD symptoms.

Another tool, the PCL, is a simple and easily administered PTSD diagnostic tool. This tool is much easier to utilize than the CAPS. However, the CAPS is a better tool to use if a clinician will be required to support his or her diagnosis to a third party (court system, insurance companies, etc.). The PCL can be completed by the client or administered by a clinician. There are 20 items on the tool measuring select PTSD criteria. Criterion B is measured by items 1 through 5, Criterion C is measured by items 6 through 7, Criterion D is measured by items 8 through 14, and Criterion E is measured by items 15 through 20. Similar to the CAPS, each symptom is scored on a range of 0 to 4. A score of 2 or greater is an endorsement for a symptom.

The last instrument, the TRS, was originally developed to measure treatment outcomes. However, it is also an effective indicator of PTSD or other trauma-related disorders. The tool's real value is that it is solution focused. The responses can be used to indicate solutions or treatment indications. The assessment comprises two parts.

Part I of the assessment is an inventory of the client's trauma. It is used to obtain a history of traumatic experiences and to indicate whether the client meets criteria for PTSD. It is only administered at intake. During Part I, the clinician attempts to develop a graphic time line of the client's life including all significant traumatic experiences. Typically, the narrative is given verbally by the client and recorded, assuming the client is comfortable with recording. The clinician and the client can later review the recording during treatment.

Part II measures treatment success and is administered repeatedly throughout treatment. The average score is representative of the client's chance of recovery. A score of 75 or greater on Part II indicates minimal traumatic distress and a significant chance of recovery. Individuals with scores lower than 75 enter the spectrum of impairment due to trauma. The lower the score, the more impaired the client, and the less successful treatment may be. Items that score less than 50 indicate an issue that should be a focus of treatment. Two items on the measure, 5a and 5b, provide an opportunity to discuss the client's feelings of safety versus his or her actual safety level.

PIDIB

The third trauma assessment, the mnemonic, PIDIB, is both an assessment and a method of rapid case conceptualization. Additionally, the model can also be used to supervise clinicians or develop treatment plans. The model includes five specific foci: establishing safety, self-stabilization, symptom management, bettering personal functioning, and reconnecting with others.

There are several benefits to the model. It can be easily utilized by clinicians of all levels, regardless the depth of the experience. Also, the model can be used to treat most individuals. Additionally, unlike other assessments, PIDIB does not require expert diagnostic ability. Application of PIDIB occurs across 5 stages.

PIDIB Stages

1. Presenting Problem
2. Issues
3. Dynamics
4. Interventions
5. Bridge

In the first stage, the client's *presenting problem* is identified. The presenting problem drives treatment planning, and must be identified before any other component of treatment. Unlike other approaches, a therapist does not need to interpret or analyze the client's statements. He or she should instead use the client's own words to restate or specify the presenting problem.

In the *issues* stage, the client's presenting problem is related to one of five specific issues: safety, control, responsibility, self-esteem, and reality testing. With this model, any presenting problem can be conceptualized as a conflict in one of the aforementioned five issues. Safety issues include both physical and psychological safety. Control issues refer to an individual's feeling out of control or being controlled by others. Also, substance abuse would be considered a control issue. Responsibility refers to an individual's blaming him or herself, or feeling guilt or shame. Self-esteem issues are self explanatory, but can be conceptualized as an individual's self worth.

The final issue is reality testing. This latter issue relates to whether or not a person is accurately experiencing reality. In this model, if a clinician suspects the client has an issue with reality testing, he or she should refer the client to a psychiatrist or a physician who can prescribe medications or medical treatment. The authors of the model developed a simple six question exam to identify issues with reality testing.

Six-Question Reality Testing Quiz

(1) Is the person hallucinating?

(2) Is the person delusional?

(3) Is the person suicidal?

(4) Is the person homicidal?

(5) Is the person using substances, alcohol, illegal drugs, or inappropriate prescription medications?

(6) Is there something strange or off-putting about the person?

The third stage is *dynamics,* referring to the therapeutic alliance between the therapist and client. It should be noted that dynamics can change between sessions, or even during a session. Some of the individual factors that impact dynamics, or relationships, are unconscious.

The fourth stage is *interventions,* and it is driven by the first three stages. A therapist reflects back upon the initial identified issue(s). The client is then empowered to choose a specific issue to begin with, resulting in the client's beginning the process of self-healing.

The final stage is *bridge*. The focus of this stage is the various bridging exercises that a counselor can provide at the beginning or end of a session. Examples include homework, connecting sessions, or self-regulation exercises.

Case Study

PIDIB

• •

This case begins with Todd's first session presenting problems. He was "sent" to therapy by his wife who threatened to leave him if he did not get help. What follows is from Todd:

I was born in Bradenton, Florida and brought up by a single mother. I am her only child. I had a wonderful childhood and was loved by an extended family. I was a good kid and never got into any trouble. All I ever really did was play ball; I was very good at sports. In fact, I was so good that I was on three varsity teams in my freshman year of high school. The other varsity players were mainly juniors and seniors and I was as good as they were. They hated that I was so young but we kept going to the state championships so they didn't say much. I began dating my high school sweetheart in my freshman year and she was also a good athlete. We hung out together, worked out together and watched each other compete. We didn't do drugs or drink or get into trouble. When I think back on it, high school was wonderful for me.

In my senior year I won a football scholarship to a Division 1 University. It was a dream come true, something I fantasized about since I was a little kid. I began working out really hard to make a good impression. I was running one day and stepped in a hole and broke my ankle in 2 places and wrecked my knee. It was awful. I needed 4 surgeries and almost a year to rehabilitate. By the time I was healed there was no scholarship. I was not a great student and didn't want to go to college – this really upset my mom.

I enlisted and served 2 tours in Iraq. The first night in Iraq I drank my first 6 pack – I didn't even know how to drink but the guys just kept handing me cans of beer and I just kept drinking. When I finished the sixth can I bent over and vomited. I couldn't stop and it was disgusting. The guys just kept laughing and I remember thinking that it was the last time I will ever drink. But from that day until yesterday and every day in between I have consumed at least one six pack. And I always drink more than a six pack and I don't always drink beer. In fact, I'll try anything that's offered.

I saw combat in both tours. Halfway through my second tour we were all waiting for a football game on TV. We were drinking and laughing and suddenly my best friend exploded all over me – he was shot by a sniper – and ever since I cannot get that memory out of my head. I go to sleep with it and I wake up with it – it's always in my head. After I was discharged I moved back with my mom. She works for the school board and got me a job there. I was fired after 2 months and my mom did not talk to me for almost a year.

I began dating my high school girlfriend and we decided to get married. She got me a job working for her father. I hate the job and I hate my father-in-law. Every day after work I go for a beer with the guys and wind up having 5 or 6. When I eventually leave for home I drive slowly and carefully and take the side streets. I have already received one DUI and if I get one more I will probably lose my license. As soon as I get home my wife is all over me, yelling at me and scolding me – I can't take it. We have a great son who is always asleep when I get home. I look in his room, give him a kiss – this kid is so beautiful – and then go into the kitchen. I make a sandwich, grab a beer and go into the den. I eat, drink, watch some porn and then pass out. When I wake up the next morning I really feel bad. I have this beautiful wife and I am a bad husband. I have this great son and I am such a bad dad. I never spend time with him and he is always asleep when I get home. I look at my reflection when I shave and say to the reflection "Todd, you are just one big loser."

What was just described above were Todd's presenting problems. His PIDIB, which identifies and validates clinical issues, was as follows:

Therapist: You said you drive home slowly and carefully after having too much to drink yet you have already had a DUI. That seems to me to be a safety issue.

Todd agreed with that statement and so we have now identified and validated one clinical issue.

Therapist: You said you go out for 1 drink and wind up having 5 or 6. That seems to suggest that there might be a control issue?

Todd agreed and so now we have identified 2 issues and validated both.

Therapist: When you wake up feeling bad because you are not being a good father or husband, you might have some issues about guilt, shame or blame?

Todd agreed and we have now identified and validated 3 issues.

Therapist: When you say to your reflection that you are one big loser, it seems to me that there is a serious self-esteem issue.

Todd agreed and we have now identified and validated 4 issues.

Once an issue has been validated it means that we can work on that issue clinically. You might notice that I did not discuss his friend being sniped. That was my clinical decision to hold off until a later session – we eventually spent many sessions on Todd's combat trauma. As you can see, this model allows you to begin work quickly with a client without having to diagnose (although diagnosing can fit into this model very well). If the client does not agree with my definition of the issues, I simply request that the client identifies the issues.

— Mike Dubi

PIDIB Model

Can you determine the PIDIB issues for Sam and Michele?

Sam is a 44-year-old male who presented for outpatient counseling. During his interview, Sam noted that he had been married previously. Two years prior, he and his then wife were in an auto accident. Sam lived through the event, but his wife did not. Though he was not driving, Sam blames himself because he was talking to her at the time and thinks he may have been a distraction. Sam reports that he drinks alone at home daily until he passes out. He claims it is the only way he can avoid thinking about his wife and his part in her death. He only came to therapy because he has been too intoxicated to go to work a few times, and is at risk of losing his job.

During the first session, his therapist Michelle identifies two presenting problems: his drinking and self blame for his wife's death. In the issues stage, his drinking is noted as a control issue and his self blame is noted as a responsibility issue. In the intervention stage, Michelle asks Sam which issue he wants to work on first. He responds with his control issue. In the bridge stage, Michelle asks Sam each week how his homework went. She also connects each intervention to their overall treatment issue.

The Trauma
Recovery Scale (TRS)

PART I

☐ Yes ☐ No I have been exposed to a traumatic event in which **both** of the following were present:

- Experienced, witnessed or was confronted with an event or events that involved actual or threatened death or serious injury, or a threat to the physical integrity of self or others, **AND**

- My response involved intense fear, helplessness or horror.

   If YES is answered please complete Part II & III; If NO is answered complete Part III (omit Part II)

PART II

Directions: Please read the following list and check all that apply.

Type of Traumatic Event	Number of Times	Dates/Age(s)		
1. Childhood Sexual Abuse	_____	_____	_____	_____
2. Rape	_____	_____	_____	_____
3. Other Adult Sexual Assault/Abuse	_____	_____	_____	_____
4. Natural Disaster	_____	_____	_____	_____
5. Industrial Disaster	_____	_____	_____	_____
6. Motor Vehicle Accident	_____	_____	_____	_____
7. Combat Trauma	_____	_____	_____	_____
8. Witnessing Traumatic Event	_____	_____	_____	_____
9. Childhood Physical Abuse	_____	_____	_____	_____
10. Adult Physical Abuse	_____	_____	_____	_____
11. Victim of Other Violent Crime	_____	_____	_____	_____
12. Captivity	_____	_____	_____	_____
13. Torture	_____	_____	_____	_____
14. Domestic Violence	_____	_____	_____	_____
15. Sexual Harassment	_____	_____	_____	_____
16. Threat of Physical Violence	_____	_____	_____	_____
17. Accidental Physical Injury	_____	_____	_____	_____
18. Humiliation	_____	_____	_____	_____
19. Property Loss	_____	_____	_____	_____
20. Death of Loved One	_____	_____	_____	_____
21. Other:_____	_____	_____	_____	_____
23. Other:_____	_____	_____	_____	_____

Comments: _____

PART III

Place a mark on the line that best represents your experiences during the past week.

1. I make it through the day without distressing recollections of past events.

|——————————————————————————————————| [ ]

0%   100% of the time

2. I sleep free from nightmares.

|——————————————————————————————————| [ ]

0%   100% of the time

3. I am able to stay in control when I think of difficult memories.

|——————————————————————————————————| [ ]

0%   100% of the time

4. I do the things that I used to avoid (e.g., daily activities, social activities, thoughts of events and people connected with past events).

|——————————————————————————————————| [ ]

0%   100% of the time

5. I am safe.

|————————————————————————| [ ]

0%   100% of the time   > [ ]

I feel safe.

|————————————————————————| [ ]

0%   100% of the time

6. I have supportive relationships in my life.

|——————————————————————————————————| [ ]

0%   100% of the time

7. I find that I can now safely feel a full range of emotions.

|———————————————————————————————————————| [ ]

0%   100% of the time

8. I can allow things to happen in my surroundings without needing to control them.

|———————————————————————————————————————| [ ]

0%   100% of the time

9. I am able to concentrate on thoughts of my choice.

|———————————————————————————————————————| [ ]

0%   100% of the time

10. I have a sense of hope about the future.

|———————————————————————————————————————| [ ]

0%   100% of the time

Scoring Instructions: record the score for where the hash mark falls on the line (0-100) in the box beside the item (average 5a with 5b to get score for 5). Sum scores and divide by 10.

Interpretation: 100–95 (full recovery/subclinical); 86–94 (significant recovery/mild symptoms); 75–85 (some recovery/ moderate symptoms); 74 (minimal recovery/severe); below 35 (probable traumatic regression)

AS – FS   **Mean Score**

[ ]   [ ]

CHAPTER 5

Tri-Phasic Model

....

Establishing Safety

COMPETENCIES IN THIS CHAPTER

- Achievement of "Good Enough" Safety and Stabilization (Phase I)

Judith Herman is a prominent author in the field of trauma. In 1992, she published *Trauma and Recovery* (Herman, 1992). the work that much of this chapter is based upon. Prior to her landmark publication, there was no unified treatment for traumatic reactions. Psychiatrists, social workers, counselors, and other professionals treated trauma in their own ways. Herman's work was a primary catalyst for the field of traumatology to become a specialized field of treatment.

In her work, she noted that there were effective treatments for traumatic reactions as far back as the 1880s, though many of those treatments were lost during the rise of psychoanalysis. She noted that in the late 19th century, clients were placed in sanitariums and allowed to convalesce. Unfortunately, these individuals did not get better. Seeing this, Pierre Janet, a French neurologist and psychologist, began changing conditions for patients. Janet had them walk around the grounds and exercise. They were also required to bathe and were provided a more nutritious diet. Janet had patients engage in structured activities throughout the day. He provided individual therapy, mostly hypnosis, and helped patients to integrate fragmented traumatic memories.

His model was *non-abreactive*, meaning individuals were not required to relive the survived experience or stay in a heightened state of emotions. Janet focused on clients remaining in a relaxed form, developing a narrative of the survived event, and healing. Though Janet's method was effective, it was supplanted by Freud's psychodynamic model.

Herman revisited Janet's work. She also explored a variety of treatments practiced prior to and through the 1980s. Herman found that effective treatments had certain commonalities and that trauma can be treated in a three phase model.

Herman's Triphasic Model

- Establishing safety
- Remembrance and mourning
- Reconnection

ESTABLISHING SAFETY

Most individuals feel a comfortable level of safety in most situations. Many clients who experience trauma, however, feel unsafe afterwards. Former feelings of safety may have diminished due to a greater awareness of perceived dangers. The goal of this initial phase of treatment is to help the client reestablish a sense of safety. This may be challenging, especially if the client is still in dangerous situations. In 1997, Gentry and Schmidt proposed 6 markers for establishing safety:

Six Empirical Markers for "Good Enough" Safety/Stabilization

(1) Resolve (real) danger

(2) Distinguish between real vs. perceived threat

(3) Develop a battery of regulation/relaxation, grounding, and containment skills

(4) Demonstrate ability to self-regulate

(5) Demonstrate ability to self-rescue

(6) Agree (verbally) to address traumatic material

Marker 1:
Resolve (real) danger

The first marker involves the client removing him or herself from actual danger. As counselors, we cannot help clients integrate traumatic memories if they are still in danger. Some examples of actual danger may include being in war zones, domestic violence situations, or even careers that hold the potential for violence, such as law enforcement or medical services. For individuals who are in real danger, the focus of psychotherapy is shifted to case management. We assist our clients in developing a safety plan and changing their lives and their environments.

For some individuals, that process may take years. For example, individuals in domestic violence situations may require a significant amount of time to learn the self-control needed to avoid conflict or to be able to leave his or her partner. If the situation includes substance abuse, more time may be needed for that treatment.

If a counselor tries to uncover traumatic memories while the client is in danger, the client may experience dissociation or a loss of connection to others in the face of violent situations. Our clients need time after a trauma treatment session to process. Clients who have to protect themselves may be putting themselves at risk by losing some of their needed cognitive functioning during the healing process. Further, our clients would continue to experience these cognitive losses in functioning in future sessions, a predicament that could leave them frequently unprepared to manage their safety. Simply put, counselors cannot limit a client's functioning when the client needs it to stay safe.

Marker 2:
Distinguish between real vs. perceived threat

The next marker involves assisting the client to differentiate between perceived danger and real danger. Again, clients who have experienced trauma often perceive danger or threats where there are none. As a result, they often feel unsafe. They may invoke behaviors, usually avoidance, to remove themselves from situations that they perceive as threatening. It is often helpful to assist clients in separating the feeling of being safe from actually being safe and real threats from perceived threats. Distinguishing between real and perceived threats is a required function in this phase, but this does not mean there are no real threats in clients' lives. Clients may need to be taught behavioral interventions to remove themselves from dangerous situations, such as recognizing danger signs, leaving a situation, and contacting the police. Our clients also need to be taught how to relax their bodies when they perceive threats. As we have seen, the only way to analyze threats with neocortical functioning is to have a relaxed body.

Marker 3:
Develop a battery of regulation/relaxation, grounding, and containment skills

The third marker involves helping our clients develop a battery of strategies for self-regulation, relaxation, grounding, containment, and expression. We should foster our clients' abilities to utilize self-regulation techniques to allow them to rescue themselves from intrusions.

Marker 4:
Demonstrate ability to self-regulate

While relaxation skills are valuable, we want to focus on teaching our clients to self-regulate in the moment and confront perceived threats. Most individuals practice relaxation skills once a day or once a week. Self-regulation is a skill that our clients can benefit from using multiple times a day as a threat is perceived.

People can only maintain frustration and anxiety for so long before it damages them. Expression strategies are focused on allowing our clients to express their inner frustrations. Such strategies allow clients to vent those feelings and energies. An example would be a giving a client a squeeze ball. The client can squeeze, shake, or even throw the ball, as long as he or she releases pent up frustration. If the client still feels frustrated, he or she can practice other expression strategies in limited bursts until the work of therapy can continue. Counselors should check in with their client between activities to ensure that there is a need and a benefit to using them and that the client isn't just losing control.

Originally noted by Baranowsky, Gentry, and Schultz (2005), the techniques described in the following paragraphs may also help a client establish safety. One technique, *diaphragmatic breathing*, is a relaxation method that, among other benefits, results in clients releasing their pelvic floor muscles. It involves asking clients to:

Diaphragmatic Breathing

1. Lace their fingers in front of their faces
2. Lean back in their chairs
3. Put their hands behind their heads
4. Pull their elbows back

The resulting physical body position forces one to engage in diaphragmatic breathing. However, some counselors and clients will choose not to use diaphragmatic breathing if body image issues come into factor, as this sort of breathing does not allow individuals to tuck in their stomachs.

Safe Place Visualization

(1) Clients are given colored sharpies and instructed to take ten minutes to draw a place that is safe and comfortable. It can be a historical site, a place the client has been before, or a place from the client's imagination. The quality of the drawing is not important, merely that a place is illustrated.

(2) Once clients are finished drawing, counselors should ask how they feel. Ideally, they answer with "safe", "comfortable", or "relaxed."

(3) Counselors should then encourage their clients by telling them that they were able to make their own safe spaces without us. If our clients can create their own safety in our offices without us, they can do it in other context of their lives.

(4) After the drawing is complete, we should ask our clients if we may approach them to see the drawing. This request demonstrates to our clients that our proximity is their own to determine, and that that we are honoring their personal space. It also demonstrates to them that we understand what it's like to be a trauma survivor. As a result, they feel understood.

(5) When we approach our clients, we need to approach to the side instead of to the front which comes off as more aggressive.

(6) We should then ask the client to explain his or her drawing.

(7) Before the client begins to talk, the counselor should interject and ask if the client would be willing to perform an experiment.

(8) Remind the client that they have had flashbacks or intrusion symptoms of traumatic events. The counselor can then ask if the client would be willing to instead develop flashbacks of safe and comfort feelings associated with the drawing.

(9) The counselor can educate the client that he or she can use this skill at any point in the future when feeling distressed.

(10) The counselor can then give the client something small to hold and encourage them to squeeze it and think about all of the good feelings, comfort, and safety associated with the drawing.

(11) After the client tells his or her story, the counselor should ask the client to carry the small object with them for the next week. Any time the client feels stressed or unsafe, he or she should touch or squeeze the object and see if any of the safety and comfort returns.

(12) Clients should then be encouraged to come back the next week and inform the counselor how the method worked.

With this technique, clients are better able to battle sympathetic nervous system dominance by relaxing their body and mind in a profound manner. This also gives them a transitional object that represents both the therapeutic process and the client's efforts.

THOUGHT FIELD THERAPY

Roger Callahan developed another technique, *Thought Field Therapy* (TFT), in the 1980s (Callahan, 2001). Callahan was one of the first modern clinicians to explore personal energy and how it affects treatment. At the time, cognitions and affect were seen at the primary treatment focus for therapy. The goal of TFT is to alter a person's energy and how it is impacting them. Callahan stated that energy moves through our body in predictable patterns through pathways called meridians. A person's energy transfer becomes blocked, deregulated, or distorted when he or she has experienced trauma, resulting in distress. The more an individual's energy becomes distorted, the more cognitive distortions there are in his or her thought field, resulting in perceptual distortions of the self and the world.

Callahan explored points in the body where energy is contained and developed a tapping sequence designed to release energy. He developed multiple sequences of body tapping, each associated with relieving different mental health conditions. One of these sequences is recommended for clients experiencing trauma and anxiety issues.

Thought Field Technique

(1) Ask your client to think about a particular distressing thought. This thought should produce anxiety, anger, fear or discomfort in the client.

(2) Develop a *Subjective Unit of Distress* score (SUDS) by asking them to assign a number to their distress between 0 and 10, with 0 being no disturbance and 10 being maximum disturbance.

(3) Teach the client to use an *algorithm*, or a unique tapping method used to treat different mental health conditions. A majority of algorithms include tapping in four spots on the body, though those spots are different depending upon the condition being treated.

(4) Once the algorithm is established, the client would complete the first 5 to 8 taps on his or her right eyebrow, the second 5 to 8 taps under his or her right eye, the third set of 5 to 8 taps 6 inches away from the right arm on the ribs, and then the fourth set of 5-8 taps about 2 inches under the collarbone on the breastplate. Afterwards, the client would attempt what is called the 9 Gamut.

(5) The 9 Gamut is a 9 sequence instructional process. Ask the client to identify their non-dominant hand and ball it into a fist. Raise balled fist in the air, clenched palm down.

(6) The client should then take the middle finger of the dominant hand and place it in the valley between the knuckles of the pinky and ring finger of the non-dominant hand.

(7) The client should then be instructed to open the closed non-dominant hand and aim their fingers outward. In the next step, the client should slowly move the middle finger toward them about an inch along the back of the non-dominant hand, resulting in the finger being rested in the valley between two metacarpals (the bones of the hand). That is the 9 Gamut spot.

The client should continually tap the 9 Gamut spot while the counselor continues to walk the client through the 9 Gamut process. The client should then be asked to sequentially:

The 9 Gamut Spot

1. Look straight ahead at me (the counselor) with your eyes open.

2. Look straight ahead at me with your eyes closed.

3. Open your eyes and keeping your head still, look down to the right.

4. Now look down to the left.

5. Now with your eyes all the way to the left of your field of vision, look all the way around in a clockwise manner.

6. Once you've completed a circle, look all the way back in another circle counter clockwise. Now look straight ahead and keep your eyes open.

7. Hum a song out loud.

8. Count to 5 out loud.

9. And hum a song out loud again.

The client would follow the 9 Gamut by tapping the four spots in sequence 5 to 8 times each. After the sequence, clients should be told to stop and take a deep breath. After they have done so, they should be asked their SUDS level again. Ideally, the SUDS level should have lowered. If the SUDS level is still high, the counselor should continue to administer the method until the SUDS is lower. Our clients should be taught that they can use this method whenever they wish to relax and manage their own anxiety. With practice, individuals do not need clinicians to administer this method.

Thought Field Therapy (TFT)

Callahan

(1) Trauma Memory

(2) SUDS

(3) Algorithm (trauma).
- Eyebrow (5-8 taps)
- Under eye (5-8 taps)
- Underarm (5-8 taps)
- Collarbone (5-8 taps)

(4) 9 Gamut
- While continously tapping 9 Gamut spot…
- Eyes open
- Eyes closed
- Eyes open down right
- Eyes open down left
- Eyes clockwise
- Eyes counterclockwise
- Hum a tune
- Count to five (aloud)
- Hum a tune

(5) Repeat #3

(6) SUDS
- If decreased 2+ units then repeat untill SUDS =0
- If decreased <2, then

(7) Psychological Reversal
- Tap on heel of hand
- "I accept myself even though I still _____" (3x)

LIGHT STREAM TECHNIQUE

Another relaxation technique, *Light Stream Technique*, is typically associated with Eye Movement Desensitization Processing (EMDR) (Shapiro, 1996).

Light Stream Technique

(1) First, ask the client where in their body they feel stress at that moment.

(2) Then ask what color they most associate with healing.

(3) Ask to imagine a column of that light color coming down from the ceiling through the part of their body where they feel stress.

(4) Encourage them to allow that light to bathe and permeate their body part for about a minute and feel its soothing ability.

(5) After the minute, ask how they feel. Hopefully, they feel more relaxed and less stressed.

ICON IN AN ENVELOPE

The *Icon in the Envelope* is another tool that can be used to help clients relax, or to close down an incomplete session where clients seem unable to lower their energy and return to normal functioning.

Icon in the Envelope

(1) Give clients a clipboard, paper, and a sharpie.

(2) Ask them to draw whatever is inside of them at the time. Clients with intrusion symptoms can also be encouraged to draw something that symbolizes the intrusive memory.

(3) After about two minutes, drawing stops with pens put down, and look at the counselor.

(4) As soon as the client puts the pen down, ask to put his or her drawing in a large envelope.

(5) Once the client has done so, the counselor should hand the client a stapler and encourage them to staple the envelope shut as many times as needed to keep it closed.

(6) The counselor then takes the envelope, writes the client's name and the date, and states, "We both know that there is more work to be done with this. We are going to get to it and resolve it. However, therapy happens here in this office with me; life happens out there. I'm going to ask you to leave this memory, this thought, this distress with me here. I will lock it in your file and hold on to the memory and the distress that goes with it. You go out there and live your life. At some point, come back here and we'll work through this and put it behind you."

(7) The counselor then puts the envelope in a drawer in front of the client.

(8) In the next session, ask if they want to work on what's in the envelope. If the client says yes, then the counselor and the client can examine the contents of the envelope. If not, then the counselor should ask if he or she could continue to keep the envelope.

(9) If the client says no, the counselor should inform the client that he or she will only bring out the envelope when the client says it is time, when the client requests it. This allows the client the freedom to stay separate from the trauma and to confront the trauma when he or she is ready.

After assisting a client in removing him or herself from unsafe internal and external situations, the next step would be to assist with the amelioration of any self-destructive thoughts or behaviors. Some clients, as a result of experiencing the traumatic event or due to symptoms of depression or other mental health conditions, will experience suicidal or homicidal behaviors or thoughts, isolate themselves, or perceive persecution or danger where there is none. A client may benefit from any number of therapies that result in lowered self-or other-harm thoughts and behaviors.

Marker 5:
Demonstrate ability to self-rescue

After a client has demonstrated the ability to self-regulate, he or she is ready to move to the next phase of the tri-phasic model. In the previous phase, clients learned how to rescue themselves from potentially dangerous internal and external situations and regulate their unsafe emotional state. But how do we as clinicians know that our clients can rescue themselves? We trigger an abreaction. An abreaction is a repressed emotion, achieved through reliving the experience that caused it.

A counselor can cause an abreaction by asking a client to describe the worst part of their most difficult, most painful trauma. Clients may initially be surprised at the question because it brings up things that are upsetting to them. However, most clients will go forward with the narrative. To bring about the abreaction, the counselor may ask for specific details of the client's narrative. Remember that we don't want our client to stay in that emotional place for very long, just long enough to start the abreaction. When the time comes to assist then, counselors can utilize the *3-2-1 sensory grounding technique*. There are several components that herald an abreaction.

Signs of an Abreaction

- All abreactions will begin with stereotypical psychomotor agitated movements, such as a leg jumping up and down. What we are seeing is a sudden rise in the client's energy level.

- Our clients will often stop when asked about it; however, they are merely containing the movement.

- As a therapist, we should encourage our clients to relax all of their muscles.

- If the client is unable to relax, his or her posture will often change to a fetal position with eyes fixed downward. The client's eyes may also widen, he or she may experience hand wringing or other forms of psychomotor agitation, and the vocal tone may rise or flatten.

- The final indicator of an abreaction is that the client may appear to dissociate, seemingly vacating their body or the situation.

3-2-1 Sensory Grounding Technique

1. The counselor should ask for the client's attention and ask, "Would you like some help to get out of there?" This question is important because it enforces the idea that individuals can save themselves. It also enforces the idea that if needed, we as counselors will be there to help them. Sometimes the knowledge that there is support will result in clients becoming more comfortable with trying to resolve their own feelings of safety.

2. If a client doesn't respond, we may lean towards them, a little off to the side so as to not be threatening, and ask, "What are you seeing right now?" The client will likely report a component of the traumatic memory.

3. The counselor should follow up with, "What organs do you see with?" When the client responds by indicating their eyes, ask them to identify three items in the room.

4. After successful completion, ask the client to name three things he or she can hear.

5. After the client denotes three sounds, the counselor should hand the client three specific objects and ask him or her to describe the texture.

6. After the client describes the texture of the objects, the counselor should ask the client to describe the differences in textures among the three items.

7. The counselor should then ask the client to name two new things he or she can hear and two new things he or she can see in the room or out the window in this moment. The counselor should then ask the client to touch and describe two new textures.

8. Finally, the counselor should then ask the client to name one thing he or she can hear, and one new thing he or she can see in the room or out the window in this moment. The counselor should then ask the client to touch and describe one new texture.

Once a client begins to experience the abreaction, the counselor can begin the 3-2-1 sensory grounding technique. The process is as follows:

Ideally, the client is no longer thinking about the traumatic event and is present enough to practice relaxation skills if needed. The client has learned how to use his or her senses to leave an emotionally upsetting place. In future sessions, counselors can remind clients that they have a tool that they can use to return them to a safe emotional place. Some clients may benefit from keeping a certain scented object that they can utilize to ground themselves when they think of the survived event. Aside from 3-2-1 Sensory Grounding, other techniques used for self-relaxation include progressive relaxation, anchoring, transitional object, postural grounding, internal vault, and timed/metered expression.

Marker 6:
Agree (verbally) to address traumatic material

The last component to be completed prior to moving forward beyond safety is to ensure that the client wants to confront his or her traumatic material. As counselors, we should not push clients to address traumatic memories. The only reason to address a traumatic memory is when the memory is preventing the client from living how he or she wishes to in the present. We should only move forward when our clients want to do so. A helpful way of ensuring this is to ask clients why processing traumatic memories would be valuable. Traumatic memories should only be explored if clients are able to justify the process to themselves, not counselors justifying the process to clients.

Thus far in this chapter, we have focused on what counselors and clients can do to ensure that the client is safe, but what qualities does a counselor require to ensure that he or she can be a healthy part of this process? A counselor has to help build and maintain a healthy therapeutic relationship: the core of any effective therapy. Also, the counselor has to maintain a non-anxious presence. As counselors, we should model relaxation skills for our clients. Any anxiety that we display may interfere with the therapeutic relationship. Staying in an anxiety state would also result in lowered neocortical functioning, which would impact our ability to connect with our clients. Finally, we must maintain positive expectancy and know that our clients can change and lead the lives that they want to.

Case Study

Helping To Create A Sense Of Safety

• •

Mark was 22 when he entered therapy. He began having nightmares several months after watching a man get beaten by a mob. By the time police arrived the man was unrecognizable due to the severity of the beating and Mark could not purge of that memory from his mind.

He remembered feeling frightened and helpless – there was nothing he could do although he wanted to help – and would then re-experience these feeling each time the memory was triggered. He said it felt as if he was reliving the actual event. He also became frightened of leaving his house and would only leave if a friend was with him. He became irritable and angry, and began smoking marijuana constantly throughout the day to help him feel better. These symptoms were typical of someone whose sense of safety was compromised – in this case by watching a beating – and he said he felt less and less safe as time went on. When he could no longer watch TV because he was afraid that something violent would pop-up on the screen, he eventually entered therapy.

Mark was able to talk about the event with minimal distress and began engaging in EMDR therapy early in treatment. EDMR therapy uses bilateral eye movements (or other bilateral stimulations) to help unfreeze the brain's information processing system. This is a brain system that is compromised during extreme stress. In addition to therapy in the office, Mark was able to create a healthy living plan to help him heal from these symptoms. The plan involved:

1. Healthy living, which included first giving up marijuana, eating a healthy diet, and regulating his sleep patterns.
2. Meditating every day. On some days he could only meditate for 5 minutes but he eventually worked up to 20 minutes.
3. Doing self-empowerment exercises such as breathing (taking a deep breath through the nose and slowly exhaling through the mouth) and bilateral tapping (from leg to leg with the palm of the hand) when he felt anxious.
4. Engaging in daily physical exercise which included running, weightlifting and martial arts training.
5. Developing safe relationships with people who validate him and make him feel good. This helps restore balance to the nervous system. One way for some people to develop safe relationships is to volunteer.

This worked well with Mark who was able to leave therapy after 6 sessions. He still sticks to his healthy living plan which has now become part of his daily routine.

Because Mark was paying for therapy himself he requested that no diagnosis be made. However, the symptoms treated were consistent with those of PTSD.

— Mike Dubi

CHAPTER 6

Tri-Phasic Model

....

Remembrance and Mourning

COMPETENCIES IN THIS CHAPTER

- Cognitive-Behavioral Method(s) that Desensitize and Reprocess Trauma Memories (Phase II)

- Reconnection Phase of Treatment (Phase III)

The first phase of Herman's tri-phasic model of treatment covered in the previous chapter is focused on helping the client establish safety. Once a client feels safe in his or her body and environment, he or she is ready to transition to the second phase of the triphasic treatment model: remembering the traumatic memory and mourning. The third phase, reconnection, is often completed at the same time as phase two. There are several methods of helping clients remember the traumatic memory. In this chapter we will explore several methods including cognitive behavioral therapy (CBT), and *eye movement desensitization and reprocessing* (EMDR).

A variety of studies have been conducted on the effectiveness of trauma treatments. One of the most thorough was the study mentioned in Chapter 1: the meta-analysis published by the Department of Veterans Affairs in 2010. One of the results of that study was a stratification of recommended treatments for PTSD. CBT and EMDR are listed in the top tier of treatments, which indicate they are strongly recommended and are sufficiently evidenced by outcome studies.

COGNITIVE BEHAVIOR THERAPIES

Cognitive behavioral therapy is a term associated with many authors. For example, Joseph Wolpe, B.F. Skinner, Ivan Pavlov, Aaron Beck, Edna Foa, Terrence Keene, Donald Meichenbaum, and Patricia Resick have all contributed to our modern use of the approach. One of these authors, Joseph Wolpe, is responsible for developing systematic desensitization. He is also an author in the field of behaviorism. He proposed that a conditioned stimulus (the sensory memory of trauma) combined with relaxation would result in extinguishing the conditioned response, or anxiety. You may recognize this *reciprocal inhibition* as one of the bases of the IATP treatment for PTSD.

CBT is a term that is used ubiquitously and sometimes incorrectly. Many clinicians practice CBT, though some of them would disagree upon its definition and principles. The National Center for Cognitive Behavioral Therapy has developed ten key concepts.

10 Key CBT Concepts

1. Our internal thoughts and feelings result in our behaviors.
2. CBT is considered a brief therapy with a limited number of sessions.
3. Maintaining a healthy therapeutic relationship is essential, but the relationship is not the focus of therapy or the resulting interventions.
4. CBT therapists maintain a collaborative relationship between the counselor and the client.
5. The philosophy upon which CBT is based is stoicism.
6. CBT therapists use the Socratic method.
7. CBT approaches are structured and directive.
8. CBT is an educational model.
9. CBT Theory and techniques rely on inductive method.
10. Homework is a central feature of CBT.

Adapted from The National Center for Cognitive Behavior Therapy key concepts

CBT Concept One:
Our thoughts cause our feelings and behaviors,
not external things such as people, situations, and events

One of the advantages to this line of thought is that we, not other people, are directly in control of our thoughts, feelings, and actions. If we change how we think, we can develop more appropriate emotional reactions.

CBT Concept Two:
CBT is considered a brief therapy with a limited number of sessions

This theory is considered to have the most rapid results for symptom reduction. An average number of sessions is 8 to 12, regardless of the client's particular issues. CBT is not a continuous process. CBT therapy has an endpoint, determined by both the counselor and client, which adds to the overall brevity of the therapy. Most modern theoretical approaches have a brief version, but that was not always true. When CBT initially came into frequent use, most therapies were long term. One of the components that results in CBT being a brief therapy is the use of homework.

CBT Concept Three:
The counseling relationship is the focus of CBT therapy

Some therapies, such as person centered therapy, focus exclusively on the client-therapist relationship. CBT therapists do not believe that the relationship is the most therapeutic aspect of treatment. With CBT, individuals progress in treatment because they change how they think and act in a way that is congruent with healthier thinking. The main focus of CBT is teaching rational self-counseling skills. Some CBT practitioners believe that the relationship develops and maintains itself automatically as a part of the process. Other CBT clinicians believe that the therapeutic relationship has to be built, and that this takes a concerted effort.

CBT Concept Four:
CBT therapists maintain a collaborative relationship between the counselor and the client

Instead of solely directing their clients, counselors elicit their client's life goals and desires. Those client-stated goals become the goals for therapy. A CBT therapist models, listens, encourages, and teaches clients, while the clients learn to think in a less distorted manner and implement that learning outside of the session.

CBT Concept Five:
The philosophy upon which CBT is based is stoicism

In general, CBT therapists do not tell clients how they should think, feel, or behave, regardless of the fact that many clients will request advice or direction. It should be noted that only some of the approaches emphasize Stoicism. Some do not. The approaches that do emphasize Stoicism focus on teaching the benefits of feeling calm when confronted with undesirable situations. They also emphasize the fact that we experience undesirable situations whether or not they upset us. While we may not be able to control the potentially distressing situation, we can control our emotional reaction to the situation. When we as individuals learn how to utilize our rational thought process we can more readily use our intelligence, knowledge, and energy to resolve problems.

CBT Concept Six:
CBT therapists use the Socratic method

We ask our clients open-ended questions to determine their wants and world views. An example would be: "What are your perceptions when your children are raising their voices at you and yelling? How are you interpreting that?" We also encourage our clients to ask themselves questions in an effort to evaluate their perceptions and judgments.

CBT Concept Seven:
CBT approaches involve a structured and directive approach

In CBT, clients decide upon their own goals. Therapists are directive in the sense that they help their clients meet self-appointed goals. A CBT therapist will have an agenda for each session, including specific techniques to teach the client.

CBT Concept Eight:
CBT is an educational model

The basis of CBT is that emotional and behavioral reactions are learned. The goal of a CBT therapist is to help a client unlearn their problematic emotional and behavioral reactions and then learn healthier ones. When people understand how and why they do things, they learn how to maintain their progress.

CBT Concept Nine:
CBT Therapists use the inductive method

A CBT therapist encourages clients to examine their thoughts as a hypothesis instead of a reality. A client should then test that hypothesis like any experiment. For example, a counselor may ask a client "does it really mean your partner doesn't love you if he walks away during an argument?" If the client's hypothesis is incorrect, then he or she can adjust to a more accurate way of thinking.

CBT Concept Ten:
Homework is a central feature of CBT

A CBT therapist trains his or her clients to question themselves in sessions. The real learning occurs when clients practice the newly learned techniques in their lives.

CBT has been evidenced to treat a variety of mental health issues. However, most CBT practices utilized to treat trauma follow a similar treatment trajectory:

CBT Treatment Trajectory

1. Assess the individual for trauma, safety issues, and other needs.
2. Stabilize the client by providing psychoeducation, relaxation techniques, training for mindfulness, and cognitive behavioral strategies to combat cognitive distortions that may lead to instability, harm to self, or harm to others.
3. Process the traumatic memory, by exposing the client to the traumatic memory (*imaginal* or *in vivo*) while maintaining a relaxed body.

Imaginal exposure occurs when an individual imagines they are in the presence of a feared object, activity, or experience. *In vivo exposure* refers to the client's directly confronting feared objects, activities, or situations, and actively engaging in those activities or situations. For example, a woman with PTSD who fears the location where she was assaulted may be assisted by her therapist in going to that location and directly confronting those fears (as long as it is safe to do so). Likewise, a person with social anxiety disorder who fears public speaking may be instructed to directly confront those fears by giving a speech. As an approach, there are quite a few benefits to the utilization of CBT. There are also concerns.

The Benefits of CBT Therapies

- Treatment can be very brief, usually 8 to 12 sessions.
- As a theoretical approach, the goals and interventions are easily measured and researched.
- The overall idea and techniques are clear and concise.
- An interested practitioner can find many books and manuals that include scripts and homework assignments.
- It is easy to find a CBT therapist.
- A counselor only requires moderate training to be proficient.

Concerns Regarding CBT Therapies

- Clients sometimes experience CBT and practitioners as "overly technical." The theoretical utilization of CBT is heavily reliant upon technical analysis of the thoughts/emotions/behaviors sequence. Additionally, some counselors new to the profession may focus heavily on using interventions without an understanding of the principles of the model.
- The intense focus on cognitions can minimize affective/emotional experiences.
- The model is therapist-driven. While the client sets goals, the therapist drives the client to meet those goals in whatever way he or she feels is appropriate. This can result in some clients feeling as though there is little collaboration. Also, this model supposes that the therapist is integral, and that a client cannot change unless a therapist directs him or her.

Techniques Utilized in CBT Therapies

- Systematic Desensitization
- Stress Inoculation Training
- Biofeedback
- Relaxation Training/Mindfulness
- Direct Therapeutic Exposure (DTE)
- Prolonged Exposure (PE)/Flooding
- Cognitive Processing Therapy
- Eye Movement Desensitization Reprocessing (EMDR)

EXPOSURE-BASED THERAPIES

As noted earlier in the chapter, the Department of Veterans affairs noted four specific evidence-based therapies for treating trauma. After CBT are exposure-based therapies, developed by Edna Foa and other authors (Foa, Hembree, & Rothbaum, 2007). Simpler versions of this therapy have been called *flooding* and *implosion*. The therapy is designed to help clients process traumatic events and reduce their PTSD symptoms as well as depression, anger, and general anxiety.

The model is practiced in three phases. Initially, the therapist provides psychoeducation about the therapeutic process and the symptoms of PTSD. Also, the autonomic nervous system, the flight or fight process, and the developmental process of trauma are explored. In the next stage, the therapist assists the client in imaginal exposure, which includes the client progressively imagining him or herself in the presence of the anxiety evoking/traumatic situation. Imaginal exposure can also occur in writing form. The client can repeatedly write a narrative of the traumatic event, filling in more detail with each authoring. In the last phase, the counselor encourages clients to practice in vivo exposure. The client engages with the feared object, situation, or person while in the presence of the counselor. The counselor helps the client to process to fear or anxiety that he or she is feeling. During this phase, clients are also actively encouraged to engage with the feared objects, people, or situations between sessions when not in the presence of the counselor as long as it is safe to do so.

Exposure therapies are very scripted and planned. A beginning therapist, or a therapist who has been practicing for years, would use the same script. Typically, a full course of treatment involves eight to 15 sessions. Also, the model is abreactive. An individual is meant to feel a range of anxiety and emotions until he or she desensitizes and can remain calm in the face of the feared objects, situations, or persons. The idea is that an individual will experience catharsis, or emotional release, and become desensitized to the memory of the traumatic event.

This type of therapy can be a very effective for people who can tolerate prolonged distress over multiple sessions. However, some people cannot tolerate that frequent level of distress.

Case Study

Abreaction

Jim was a 35-year-old small business owner who was referred by his wife, who threatened to leave him if he did not see a therapist. The problem he presented had to do with his wife's discomfort when he looked at other women in his daily activities. This was, in fact, a serious problem because there was no way Jim could function without looking at women while at work or watching TV or in a restaurant. The therapist was not sure about what he was being asked to treat.

As Jim was talking to the therapist, he suddenly had a powerful abreaction. He began sweating, breathing heavily and gasping for air. His speech was labored and he kept gasping as he cried, "he's on my chest, I can't breathe," … "I can't breathe please get off my chest" and then he began choking and crying. Jim was allowed to process the abreaction and when he was back to his normal baseline he shared the following story:

Jim's father was an Air Force General who moved the family to an upscale beach community upon retirement. His father was also a cross dresser who walked around the house in ladies' sexy underwear. His mother was an alcoholic who was distant from Jim and his father. Jim's father built a shed in the backyard which he locked and told Jim never to go into.

Jim was 9 at the time and, of course, somehow managed to get into the shed. When he first entered, he just looked around at the sexy underwear, sex toys and magazines – he was confused and not sure what he was actually seeing but knew it was bad; the next thing he felt was his father's hand on the back of his shirt. His father dragged him onto the lawn, knocked him down and sat on his chest with his knees holding down his arms. Jim believes that his father tried to sexually abuse him but is not sure. What did happen was that it became a repressed memory almost as soon as the event ended and Jim had no memory of the event until he came into therapy at his wife's insistence.

Jim and his therapist spent several sessions on his relationship with his father, especially the sexual abuse the sessions revealed and his anger towards his father and his mother.

— Mike Dubi

COGNITIVE PROCESSING THERAPY

Cognitive processing therapy was originally designed by Patricia Resick to treat victims of sexual assault (Resick & Schnicke, 1993). It has become more sophisticated over time and now is a model favored by the Department of Veterans Affairs for treating combat-related PTSD. It is a scripted model of therapy, occurring over 12 sessions unless the client has a loss or bereavement issue associated with the trauma. If so, the total number of sessions is 13.

Session Order for Cognitive Processing Therapy

- Session 1 - Introduction and Education
- Session 2 - The Meaning of the Event
- Session 3 - Identification of Thoughts and Feelings
- Session 4 - Remembering Traumatic Events
- Session 5 - Identification of Stuck Points
- Session 6 - Challenging Questions
- Session 7 - Patterns of Problematic Thinking
- Session 8 - Safety Issues
- Session 9 - Trust Issues
- Session 10 - Power/Control Issues
- Session 11 - Esteem Issues
- Session 12 - Intimacy Issues and Meaning of the Event:
- Session 13 - Bereavement Processing (if loss)

The model uses the ABC sequence similar to that of CBT. A is the activating event. B is the individual's belief(s) about the event. C is the emotional consequence.

Four Main Components of Cognitive Processing Therapy

(1) Learning about the symptoms of PTSD and the ABC sequence.

(2) Becoming aware of problematic thoughts and feelings.

(3) Learning skills to change automatic thoughts and reactions.

(4) Understanding changes in beliefs.

To complete the process, clients are expected to write an impact statement: a narrative of the trauma and how it has impacted them. Each subsequent session includes a focus on further developing the narrative, becoming desensitized to the trauma, integrating memories, evaluating perceptions, and pursuing more beneficial beliefs.

STRESS INOCULATION TRAINING

The third recommended treatment, Stress Inoculation Training was developed by Donald Meichanbaum in the 1970s (Meichenbaum & Cameron, 1989). It was originally developed as a tool to manage anticipatory anxiety in situations like public speaking or test taking. Over time, it has matured to be used for other applications. The model places more emphasis on breathing retraining and muscle relaxation, but also includes cognitive elements (self-dialogue, thought stopping, role playing) and often, exposure techniques (in-vivo exposure, narration of traumatic event).

Stress Inoculation Training

- The individual is asked to identify the anxiety provoking situation.
- The counselor asks the client to report their level of anxiety on a scale.
- The counselor provides details of the scenario to better help the client visualize and place him or herself in the scenario.
- The counselor then assists the client in relaxing their body while continuing imaginal exposure of the anxiety provoking scenario.
- The client eventually reaches a maximum level of anxiety and begins to calm down due to desensitization.

EYE MOVEMENT DESENSITIZATION AND REPROCESSING

The final method recommended by the Department of Veterans Affairs is eye movement desensitization and reprocessing (EMDR). Originally developed by Frances Shapiro in the 1980s, it is frequently utilized for the treatment of trauma (Shapiro, 1989). The model is used by over 60,000 licensed mental health therapists located in 52 countries.

EMDR is an integrated model that draws from behavioral, cognitive, psychodynamic, body-based, and systems therapies. EMDR has been evidenced in a variety of studies to provide profound and stable treatment effects in a short period of time. It is worth noting that there are more controlled studies to date on EMDR than on any other method used in the treatment of trauma. Also, EMDR is the only well-researched treatment model capable of addressing multiple traumatic incidents simultaneously.

Treatment typically occurs across eight phases and 11 steps that include the use of eye movement and other bilateral stimuli, and evoking traumatic associations. As a result, any fragmented memories enter into consciousness and become integrated. This process occurs across a revolving sequence. First the client visits the traumatic memory for a moment and then the counselor processes this memory with the client. The client then returns to the traumatic memory and so on. As this process repeatedly occurs, the client becomes more proficient at entering a traumatic memory and then returning to the present, evidencing more desensitization.

The first three phases are focused on safety and stabilization. Traumatic memory processing occurs in the middle three phases. Finally, the last two phases focus on re-experiencing. In her work, Shapiro describes EMDR as an accelerated information processing model. An EMDR clinician does not assume the client is experiencing pathology. Instead, survivors are in the process of adapting and self-healing. Also, EMDR is said to facilitate and accelerate this self-healing. According to this model, thwarted self-healing is the cause of traumatic symptoms.

Bilateral stimulation assists with the processing of traumatic material. The method can be utilized to facilitate relaxation, distract the client from experiencing the trauma, diminish the individual's capacity for repression and inhibition, and increase the client's focus. EMDR is multimodal, meaning that it utilizes a variety of treatment modalities; it includes cognitive, behavioral, somatic, schematic, affective, and self-assessment components. This method is also client driven and allows for all forms of bilateral stimulation. EDMR is noted to be as effective as CBT, but with a quicker resolution and a lower dropout rate. The model is applied in 11 steps.

The Eleven Steps of EMDR

(1) Situation: The client is asked the situation he or she wants to work on.

(2) Target: The client is then asked to target a time in the past month when the negative experience has been experienced the most.

(3) Negative Cognition/Self-referencing Belief: The client is asked to recall the target image and provide some words that represent the negative belief that the client has in him or herself.

(4) Positive Cognition/Self-referencing Belief: The client is asked to create a belief about him or herself in the context of this target memory.

(5) Validity of Cognition (VOC): The client is asked to apply the positive belief to the mental image and to provide a response how accurate it feels on a one to seven scale, with seven being the highest.

(6) Emotions: The client is asked to think of his negative belief and state the emotions that he or she feels in connection.

(7) Subjective Units of Distress (SUDs): The client is asked to rate how distressing his or her emotions are on a scale of one to ten, with ten being the highest.

(8) Body Scan: The client is asked where he or she feels stress in the body.

(9) Desensitization (Bilateral stimulation while processing target): The client is asked to think of the target memory and the negative belief and keep his or her eyes on the tip of the counselor's pen or finger. The counselor then waves his pen/finger from right to left. The client reports any effects felt. The counselor then alternates between a minute of bilateral stimulation and a minute of processing until the client reports an effect. The process may require a few cycles.

(10) Installation

(11) Body Scan/Homework/Journal

Throughout the process, clients continue to make associations with their trauma and become desensitized. The process is repeated multiple times in a session and across multiple sessions until the client no longer feels a need for treatment.

Case Study

EMDR Treatment

• •

Tanya was 21 when she participated in therapy but her therapy was only one 90-minute EMDR therapy session.

From the age of 7 until she was 21, Tanya was sexually abused by her step-father who also produced pornographic movies of her which he sold worldwide. He told Tanya that he was a member of the Mafia and if she told anyone he would make her watch as he slowly tortured her mother to death. He said that after killing her mother he would slowly torture her to death as well.

When she was 21, Tanya got a job at a local supermarket as a cashier and she began dating a young man, Bill, who worked with her. After several months Bill proposed marriage. She then told Bill the story of her abuse. Bill and Tanya went to the step-father to tell him of their marriage and that the abuse was over. The stepfather replied "Over? Bill, I'm going to make you a movie star as well."

Bill and Tanya then went to the local woman's shelter who immediately admitted her but not Bill because shelters are created to provide safety for women. The next morning, Tanya had to appear in court and went with the shelter's advocate and attorney. As they entered the court room, Tanya saw the step-father sitting in the gallery and fainted. Everyone in the court room witnessed the fainting incident. That night the therapist received a phone call from the Director of the shelter explaining what had happened in court. She told the therapist that Tanya would have to appear in court the following week to testify against the step-father and was concerned that Tanya would faint again.

The therapist and client engaged in one EMDR session and Tanya responded quite well to the treatment. Using bilateral stimulation Tanya was able to process and desensitize the memories that overwhelmed her in court a few days earlier.

The following week the therapist received a call from the Director who was amazed at the results. She said, "When Tanya walked into the courtroom with her attorney and the advocate, she had to pass the table where her step-father and his attorney sat. As she approached the step-father's table she stopped, leaned in and said to the stepfather 'I'm taking you down today.'" Everyone in court who had seen Tanya faint the previous week was amazed at the difference. The step-father's computers were brought into evidence and he changed his plea to guilty and negotiated and a plea bargain.

Not all EMDR therapy is as brief as one session, of course, but they do tend to be briefer than most other forms of psychotherapy.

— Mike Dubi

CATEGORY C AND I TREATMENTS

Up until this point in this chapter, we have explored evidence-based treatments recommended by the Department of Veterans Affairs as Category A, top tier treatments. Category C treatments have some evidence to support their application but no real recommendation for use. Category C contains patient education, imagery rehearsal therapy, psychodynamic therapy, hypnosis, relaxation techniques, and group therapy.

A number of therapies involve *patient education*. There are several goals to providing education about diagnosis and treatment. Many clients are more hopeful of the success of trauma treatment simply by being educated about potential treatment outcomes. Clients are also better able to advocate for themselves with you and other professionals if they understand their diagnosis and needs. Clients may also be more compliant with treatment, with fewer treatment complications, once they understand the goals and methods of trauma treatment.

Image rehearsal therapy (Barrett, 1996) is a cognitive behavioral technique. It is utilized to reduce the frequency and severity of nightmares associated with PTSD. The therapy typically involves clients being trained to monitor their nightmares and later, recalling their nightmare in session while providing a different, less upsetting ending. While in session, clients will continue to mentally revisit each nightmare with the altered ending.

Clinicians who practice *psychodynamic therapy* believe that traumatic memories and thought processes that we are unaware of, that are located in our unconscious, result in psychic tension or traumatic stress. The goal for a psychodynamic therapist is to bring the unconscious memories to the conscious level, where clients can process them, and better understand their influence on past and present behavior.

Similarly, *hypnosis* is a technique often utilized in psychodynamic therapy. Hypnosis involves reducing the client's focus on their present peripheral awareness, focusing their attention on a memory or situation, and increasing their capacity for suggestion. With trauma treatment, hypnosis is often utilized to better help a client recall a traumatic memory that the client may not be able to recall on their own without anxiety.

Regardless of theoretical approaches, most clinicians teach some form of *relaxation techniques*. Many of our clients feel a heightened degree of anxiety and tension due to their trauma or mental health issues. By themselves, relaxation techniques are often utilized to help clients release tension. Relaxation techniques are often used with trauma treatments as a way to reduce the client's anxiety while he or she recalls and processes traumatic memories.

Group therapy is another treatment utilized for a variety of mental health issues. The process involves treating multiple clients at the same time. Psychoeducation is often a primary treatment method utilized with group therapy. Ideally, clients learn about themselves from the group leader and the experiences of other group members. Any number of skills can be taught and practiced in group therapy: mindfulness, anger management, relaxation training, social skills, etc. With trauma treatment, the focus of group therapy is processing traumatic experiences, practicing relaxation skills, and sharing support for moving forward.

Category I treatments have no evidence supporting their application. Therapies included in Category I are family therapies, web-based CBT, acceptance and commitment therapy, and dialectical behavioral therapy.

Family therapy is a dual concept. On one hand, many theoretical approaches have been modified to treat an entire family unit. On the other hand, a variety of theoretical approaches have been developed to use exclusively with families. Trauma focused family therapies aim to assist a family in processing a traumatic memory or a loss, and moving forward with their lives.

Web-based CBT is another Category I treatment. The model includes the same tenets and basic practices of cognitive behavior therapy. However, the mode of delivery is by an internet program instead of face-to-face with a practitioner. Further, treatment is provided by weekly modules that are a combination of self-help and psychoeducation. Depending upon the program, there can be little to no direct therapist involvement.

The focus of ***acceptance and commitment therapy*** (ACT) (Hayes, Strosahl, and Wilson, 2012) is not to be happy, but rather to be mindful of our current lives and circumstances. A clinician utilizing ACT teaches a combination of acceptance and mindfulness strategies. When used to treat trauma, the focus is to bring the client's focus and attention to the present, instead of focusing on the traumatic event which is in the past.

Dialectical behavior therapy (DBT) (Linehan, 1999) is another modified form of cognitive behavioral therapy. The initial treatment population for this therapy was individuals with borderline personality disorder, individuals who self-harmed, expressed suicidal thinking, or abused drugs. However, the approach has been applied to a broader spectrum of clients with a wider range of mental health issues. The goal is to assist clients with more effective regulation of their emotions, tolerating distress more easily, and self-acceptance. When treating trauma, the focus is increasing the self-regulation skills of clients reporting depression and anxiety. Another focus is helping the client exist in the present.

CHAPTER 7

The IATP Narrative Exposure Therapy

. . . .

COMPETENCIES IN THIS CHAPTER

- Cognitive-Behavioral Method(s) that Desensitize and Reprocess Trauma Memories (Phase II)

The International Association of Trauma Professionals (IATP) narrative exposure therapy is a structured sequential model that includes the development of a graphic timeline, a written timeline, a pictorial narrative, a verbal narrative, and a recursive narrative. The use of the timelines and various narratives are an integration of several methods, including trauma-focused CBT, EMDR, cognitive processing therapy, traumatic incident reduction, and prolonged exposure.

Many models of trauma treatment focus on releasing emotions during the memory processing experience. However, that release can often interfere with a client being able to recall or express the memories. The aforementioned techniques are utilized sequentially to process memories and integrate them in a manner that is non-abreactive. A client is encouraged to first describe the incident in a graph, then as a picture, and then verbally. As a progression, a client moves from recalling the traumatic event, to drawing it, to being able to verbalize the event: a task that is challenging for many clients. In combination, the techniques serve as an excellent tool for helping survivors have a positive mastery experience when confronting traumatic memories. The techniques themselves are highly structured but easy to utilize. The therapy is typically administered over the course of one 50-minute session; however, the process should be explained and set up in the prior session.

Narrative One:
Graphic Timeline Exercise

The first step in the IATP model is developing a graphic timeline of the traumatic event. The exercise itself should be introduced in one session and reviewed in the next so that the client has time to complete the majority of the assignment as homework.

The timeline itself should be constructed from when the client first perceived a threat (the beginning point) to when the client realized that he or she would survive (the end point).

In the first session, the to when the client realized that he or she would survive (the end point). In the first session, the counselor should explain the technique. The counselor should also provide a low intensity example of completing the timeline before asking the client to complete the timeline. The goal of this technique is for the client to provide a structure to the traumatic event. This introductory session should require no more than 15 to 30 minutes.

Graphic Timeline Exercise

The counselor should:

1. Provide the client with a large sheet of paper and ask him or her to write/draw the survived events in chronological order along a timeline.
2. Encourage the client to describe or write the beginning and end points of the survived experience during this introductory session.
3. Afterwards, instruct the client to take the assignment home and write in the events that occurred in the middle.

*Note: Some counselors may choose to specifically encourage their clients to denote the worst part of the timeline.

Some clients may have a difficult time deciding when the end point occurred. An easy way to help the client decide this is to ask them when they felt they could sleep. An individual has to relax; their SNS has to disengage, in order to sleep. If an individual is a in a prolonged event that occurs for several days, the endpoint of the graphic timeline is the first time he or she falls asleep.

The following graphic timeline represents a completed timeline for a client who was involved in an auto accident. As you will note, being in the automobile (Nissan) serves as the beginning point, which is the point where the client felt danger. Being checked out by the EMT serves as the end point, or the point where the client knew he or she would survive.

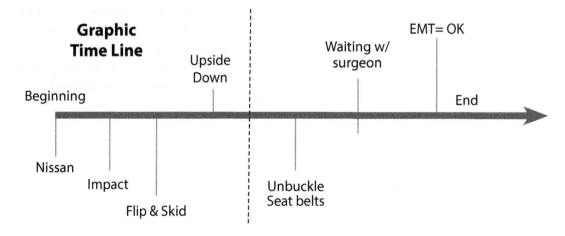

In the next session, the counselor should review the timeline with the client. If the client reports that he or she was not able to complete the timeline for any reason, this is an indicator that the client may not be ready to work through the memory. The counselor should ask if the client is ready to resolve the memory, but he or she should not coerce the client. Remember that at this phase, counselors should not be forcing the client to confront traumatic material. However, there should previously have been some discussion with the client about the memories of past trauma intruding upon the client's perceptual view of the present, and the benefits of treatment in the here and now. If a client is not ready to complete the timeline, the counselor should work with him to ensure that the treatment goals of trauma memory resolution are still appropriate.

Assuming the client completed the graphic timeline, the counselor should congratulate the client for completing a difficult task. After all, completion of the graphic timeline exercise may serve as the first time a client has been able to successfully recall and express the traumatic memory. After a client has successfully completed and explained the graphic timeline, he or she should attempt the next component: the written narrative.

Narrative Two: Written Narrative

The goal of the written narrative is to have a client write a narrative of the traumatic event. The exercise is comprised of two parts with an intermission in between. Each half is relatively short, usually around 5 minutes. This should transition directly from the completed graphic timeline exercise.

Written Narrative

1. Have the client put a dot in the middle of the graphic timeline. Ask the client to develop a written narration from the beginning of the graphic timeline to this middle point.

2. Make sure your client remains relaxed during this exercise. Remind the client, "What should you be doing while writing this timeline?" Ideally, the client will respond by indicating they should keep their body relaxed. Remember, if individuals are not relaxed, they may re-traumatize themselves by recalling the memory. Also, staying calm while recalling the traumatic memory will help desensitization, the goal for our clients.

3. The client should be given about five minutes to complete the first part of the written narrative.

4. While he or she is writing, observe the client. If you notice some form of psychomotor agitation, such leg-jumping, interrupt the client and encourage him or her to remain in a relaxed body. A client who stays agitated for even 10 seconds may not be able to complete the exercise.

5. When the client initially shows signs of agitation, provide a cue, such as a loud sigh or deep breath, to orient the client to the present and lower his or her agitation. If that method is ineffective, state the client's name and ask for their attention. You can then encourage the client to stay relaxed. During the first half of the writing process, provide verbal prompts, roughly about every 90 seconds, such as, "Keep your body relaxed," or, "With a relaxed body take two more minutes." Once the client has finished the first half of her narrative, assist her in practicing a relaxation skill such as diaphragmatic breathing. Relaxing at this juncture also serves to bring the client back to the present for a moment.

6. Once the client is relaxed again, ask him to resume writing the second half of his written narrative. The final product should be a written narrative of the entire traumatic event.

> ## Case Study
>
> ## Written Narrative
>
> •
>
> **Using the previous example, an abbreviated written narrative may look like the following:**
>
> I was riding in my new Nissan in the afternoon. I had just left work. I remember being hit by another car. It hit me on my side, the driver's side. I remember the impact, and then the car was upside down. I remember the sound the roof made on the pavement. I was upside down next, but I was hanging. My seatbelt was holding me in.
>
> I panicked for a minute because I couldn't get it undone. After a few moments, it finally opened and I fell to the ground. I crawled out the window. It was easy because it was broken. When I finally sat upright, my knee hurt. I thought it was broken. Someone from the sidewalk rushed up and asked if I was ok. Someone else called 911. I sat with the person who had rushed up to me for a few moments. I heard the ambulance before I saw them. When they pulled up, an EMT walked over and began to check me out. After a few moments of conversing with the EMT, I knew I was going to be ok. When I got to the hospital they treated the cut on my knee and released me.
>
> — Eric Gentry

Once a client has completed the written narrative, he or she should be encouraged to attempt the pictorial narrative. Each type of narrative is meant to assist the client in remembering either new details or the event as a whole. The pictorial narrative may be useful for people who learn or express themselves visually.

Narrative Three:
Pictorial Narrative

After the written narrative, the counselor should transition the client into the pictorial narrative by giving him or her a pictorial narrative template. The counselor should request that client draw six images from the story that he or she has just written. Clients are encouraged to begin by drawing the beginning- and end-points first, and then complete four drawings in the middle. This exercise requires about ten minutes at the most. Clients should also be informed that their artistic skill does not matter and will not be judged. This type of narrative can be very beneficial because the method elicits the sensory non-verbal components of the traumatic memory. Again, counselors should assist clients in maintaining a relaxed body about every 2 minutes.

The following is an example of the pictorial narrative using the previous examples:

As you can see, pictorial representations of components of the traumatic events have been illustrated. Ideally, the client has illustrated the most important or tangible components of the traumatic event. Once the client has completed the pictorial narrative, the counselor should transition the client to performing the verbal narrative.

Narrative Four:
The Verbal Narrative

The goal of the verbal narrative is for a client to be able to verbalize the traumatic event. Again, this may be the first time a client has verbalized events, so he or she may find it difficult. The instructions for the exercise are fairly simple.

The Verbal Narrative

1. After the client completes the drawing, ask, "May I approach you?"
2. After approaching the client, ask him or her to use the picture to tell their story while trying to remain relaxed.
3. Do not interrupt the narrative unless the client experiences emotional deregulation and requires calming interventions.
4. Once the verbal narrative is complete, thank the client for letting you have the honor of receiving that story.

The verbal narrative process should take no more than 15 minutes. Afterwards, assist the client in the final narrative, the recursive narrative.

Narrative Five:
Recursive Narrative

The goal of the verbal narrative was for the client to verbally narrate his or her traumatic memory, and to be able to hear the narrative and place him or herself within that story. While some clients may be able to verbalize the traumatic events, it is often harder to hear the story and place themselves in them. Like the verbal narrative, the instructions for this technique are simple.

The Recursive Narrative

1. After hearing the verbal narrative, ask, "May I see your pictures (pictorial narrative)?"
2. Retell the client's narrative as accurately as possible without embellishing, using the same language and inflections that the client used.
3. During the retelling, speak in the third person and use the client's name and gender-specific pronoun.
4. Model a decreased level of anxiety when telling the story by keeping a relaxed body.

After the client has successfully completed all parts of the exercise, the counselor should limit the level of input they provide while being careful to not appear dismissive, such as putting a one or two sentence spin or flourish on the immersive experience. Give the client 5 or 10 minutes to discuss the experience. This process may be challenging for some clients as they may experience an array of emotions after telling their story. If a client is escalated, he or she may benefit from diaphragmatic breathing or counting backwards from 100 by sevens. Ideally, this process brings the client's thoughts to the present and assists with regulating the ANS.

Clients should be encouraged to practice aerobic activities after the session to release anxiety. Counselors should probe for supports and encourage the client to use them. Support will benefit clients who may be vulnerable after recalling the traumatic memories. Some clients will re-experience the event after the session simply due to talking about it. Clients should be told that if they re-experience after 36 hours, or their anxiety does not dissipate within 72 hours, they should contact you.

Every session of remembering should be followed by a session of processing. Alternating between uncovering sessions and processing sessions should continue until the client has no further traumatic memories to integrate. Some individuals will have experienced multiple traumata. The IATP model of utilizing the graphic timeline and the three narratives can also be utilized over a large period of traumatic time, such as a person's lifespan or a long sequence of traumata.

CHAPTER 8

Grief, Loss, and Mourning

....

- Resolve the Grief and Other Peripheral Issues Accompanying Treatment of PTSD

Many individuals who experience trauma have also experienced loss. A loss can come in many forms: loss of sense of security, wealth, physical ability, and identity, loss of a close individual, and so on. A loss can be devastating to a client; however, grief should not be viewed as pathology. This is not to say that there are not diagnosable conditions that arise from grief. For example, major depressive disorder may sometimes be associated with grief. Grieving is a natural process. It is our way of healing ourselves and moving forward. A grieving individual does not always require treatment. Most people are perfectly capable of healing themselves from loss without clinical intervention. As long as our clients are not harming themselves or others, our responsibility as clinicians is to help them with their organic healing process. In a case where an individual is causing, or threatening to cause, harm to himself or others, we must intervene for safety.

Worden (2008), a known author in the field of grief, summarized the grieving process by stating, "Grieving allows us to heal, to remember with love rather than pain. It is a sorting process. One by one, you let go of things that are gone. You mourn for them. One by one you take hold of the things that have become part of who you are and build again."

GRIEF COUNSELING SUPPORT

For counselors, there are five main components to supporting individuals who are grieving.

Five Components to Grief Support

(1) Listening

(2) Developing and maintaining the therapeutic relationship

(3) Providing psychoeducation

(4) Providing case management

(5) Assisting the client with self-regulation

A counselor may be the first person, and sometimes the only person, that a client will have to talk to about his or her loss. Prior to entering the counseling relationship, a client may not have the option to talk to family or friends without causing too much pain for all parties. For a client to be able to express a narrative, the most essential component is to have a counselor who will *listen* without judgment or restriction to the client.

Supporting Grief Component One:
Listening

A counselor may be the first person, and sometimes the only person, that a client will have to talk to about his or her loss. Prior to entering the counseling relationship, a client may not have the option to talk to family or friends without causing too much pain for all parties. For a client to be able to express a narrative, the most essential component is to have a counselor who will *listen* without judgment or restriction to the client.

Remember: listening is not talking. **As counselors, we aren't providing interventions or directions**. We listen to our grieving clients so that they can verbally process the loss. As counselors and human beings, it is easy to feel threatened by an emotional client, causing a part of us to feel the instinctual need to act. Remember, as our SNS activates, we lose some of our neocortical functioning. However, if we act or provide an intervention to ameliorate our own anxiety, we diminish our client's ability to tell that narrative. Also, if we offer a question at every moment of silence, we begin to foster a dependency that disrupts the narrative. When listening, we ideally should maintain a pleasant look on our faces and nod at our clients to go on.

Supporting Grief Component Two:
Developing and maintaining the therapeutic relationship

Building a healthy therapeutic relationship with the client is another, and likely the most important, component. Clients need an environment where they feel heard and sufficiently safe to produce their narrative. While listening is very valuable, it is only one component of a relationship. A client may need to feel that he or she shares a connection with a counselor, and that said counselor has a vested interest in the relationship and in the well-being of the client. Counselors should utilize their own personal and clinical skills to develop relationships with their clients. Session rating scales, such as the SRS mentioned in Chapter 3, and other tools can also be beneficial for counselors to improve relationships with clients. The use of feedback informed therapy allows for counselors to build relationships with clients over time.

Supporting Grief Component Three:
Providing Psychoeducation to Grieving Clients

Providing psychoeducation is a therapist's main technique or intervention when helping a grieving client. Many of our clients seek a specific treatment when they begin grief therapy. As counselors, we must educate them that there is no treatment for grief, because grief is not pathology. Grieving is a natural process that there is no way to avoid. The clients have experienced significant emotional and physical wounds, and there is no healthy way to avoid the healing process, regardless of how uncomfortable it may be. If clients do choose to avoid the grieving process, we should inform them that they are likely to experience emotional ramifications for the rest of their life.

Some clients may come to therapy because they do not understand some of their thoughts, feelings, or why they can't "get over it and move on." They may not understand why moving on appears so easy for others in comparison to themselves. These clients will need to be educated how grieving affects individuals, and how the process is different for everyone. Many clients will also need to be educated about the symptoms of grief, such as depression, potential self-harm thoughts, fatigue, and other associated symptoms. Finally, our clients need to be educated about how therapy can support them in the grieving process. Remember: *supporting* a client during grieving is *not treating* the client.

Supporting Grief Component Four:
Providing Case Management

Case management may be a component of some clients' therapy. When individuals grieve, they often lose their sense of belonging and their drive to manage their lives. These individuals may subsequently have lowered performances at work or in school. They may become unable to take care of themselves or family members, or to arrange and attend counseling, medical, or other health appointments. A clinician may have to serve as a case manager and assist the client in maintaining their needs and moving forward with their lives. Counselors may also recommend ancillary services, such as local support groups, or social service agencies that may be beneficial to the client.

Supporting Grief Component Five:
Assisting the Client With Self-regulation

Many of our clients will feel unable to regulate their depression or anxiety symptoms, resulting in heightened negative emotional states. The client may need to be taught about the ANS and regulation and relaxation strategies so that he or she can process grief and minimize avoidance. Again, this is not a treatment, this is teaching a developmental skill that can be used in a variety of situations.

In order to better understand how self-regulation benefits clients, one should understand the difference between normal and complicated grief. One of the most significant differences between the two are the symptoms that occur with complicated bereavement, which are suffering, depression, and avoidance. Grief can be thought of as a wave with a peak point where emotional pain is at its highest, and a trough where the individual has become desensitized to grief and is in the recovery process.

The following graph indicates a normal grieving process. When an individual initially experiences grief, he or she experiences a rising level of energy associated with the loss. That energy continues to rise until it reaches a maximum point, usually accompanied by crying and other signs of acute grief. Once individual is able to bodily relax, he or she becomes desensitized to the pain or the loss and integrates it into his or her consciousness. This then returns the individual to a momentary pre-loss level of energy.

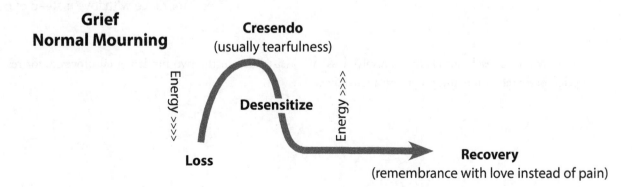

Assuming that an individual is able to retain a relaxed body, future episodes will still cause him or her to experience a rise in energy. However, the period of time remaining at that high level of energy will be shortened and the intensity of the energy will be lessened. As a result, each successive time the individual experiences a rise in energy, it will occur for shorter periods of time and with less intensity.

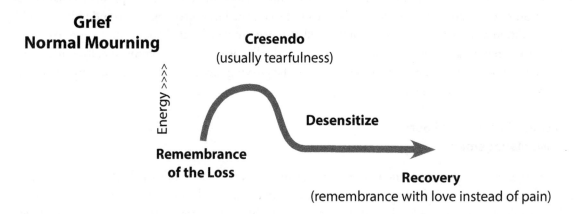

Some individuals, however, may avoid processing loss or grief, resulting in complicated bereavement and mourning. The human mind will always continue to try to heal itself from grief. The more the mind fails in that attempt, the more an individual may become demoralized and hopeless. If we suppress the grief every time our brain brings the loss back to consciousness, we become demoralized and overwhelmed. This may cause some grieving individuals to stay at a heightened point of emotional energy much longer than others. They may also feel heightened degrees of depression, hopelessness, and emotional suffering. The behavior of repeatedly causing this heightened degree energy and emotional response is called *rumination*. If clients are unable to relax their bodies, they may not reach a real level of desensitization or resolution. An individual feeling muscle tension and anxiety has the tendency return to high levels of emotional energy because they can't desensitize in a normal manner.

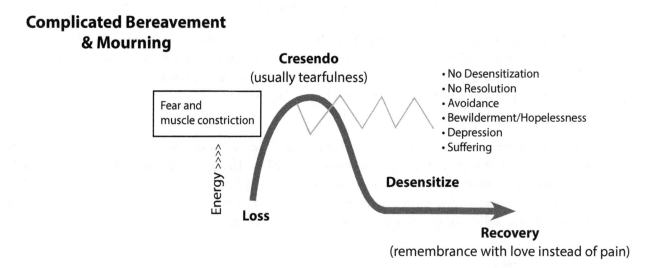

So how do we teach our clients to resolve loss? We assist them in the two fundamental processes for resolving grief: body relaxation and providing a narrative.

PROBLEM TO SOLUTION

Relaxation

Remembrance of Loss + Relaxed Body = Desensitization and Lessening of Pain

---

Narrative

Telling Story of Loss (Eulogy) + Relaxed Body = Relegating Loss to the Past + Remembering with Love
(instead of Pain)

A key focus should include helping clients to remember their losses while maintaining a relaxed body. This can lead to less physical and mental anguish, a greater sense of desensitization, and an integration of the loss. Another key component includes developing a narrative that includes telling the story of the loss, relegating it to the past, and remembering the lost person with love. By developing a narrative, our clients are integrating their memories and their losses.

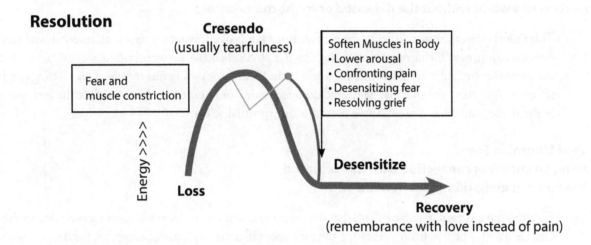

Once individuals learn how to relax their bodies, they have a greater chance to lower their arousal level, desensitize their reaction to the memory of the loss, and focus on resolving grief.

THE TASKS OF MOURNING

Mourning, or accepting loss, means integrating the loss into one's life and continuing to live. This is a natural component of life, but it is not always an easy task. Worden noted four specific tasks for mourning that individuals have to complete.

Tasks of Mourning

1. Accepting the reality of the loss.
2. Processing the pain of grief.
3. Adjusting to a world without the deceased or to a material loss.
4. Finding an enduring connection.

Task of Mourning One:
Accepting the reality of the loss

We must avoid minimizing or suppressing the loss. This can be challenging because some losses are so monumental that it may be hard for a client to even consider a life without what has been lost. For example, a recent widow who was married for 30 years may find it challenging to accept that she no longer has her husband. Likewise, a parent who has raised a child for 18 years may find it difficult to accept that the child has died, or has moved out of the home.

Task of Mourning Two:
Processing the pain of grief

Processing is externalizing that pain, developing a narrative, and sharing it. Many of our clients will make attempts to avoid or ignore the loss because of the emotional pain caused by remembering. Our clients eventually have to process that pain, along with the memory of the loss, in order to accept the loss, integrate the memory of the person, and move forward.

Task of Mourning Three:
Adjusting to a world without the deceased or to the material loss

This task is often the most difficult. People face three kinds of adjustments: external, internal, and spiritual. The external adjustment includes making changes to the physical and social world where we interact with others and our environment. Adjusting the internal world includes understanding our thoughts and feelings and how they affect us. Adjusting the spiritual world includes realigning our spiritual selves to reflect the loss, our new place in the world, and what those changes mean for our spiritual selves.

Task of Mourning Four:
Finding an enduring connection with the deceased
in the midst of embarking on a new life

Even though a person may have died, that does not mean our clients have lost their connections to the deceased. Our clients may benefit from celebrating the time spent together and maintaining that connection in one form or another. An enduring connection may take many forms including keeping photos of the deceased, telling stories about the deceased, talking to the deceased (with the recognition that the person has died), or other forms.

Three Steps to Grief Resolution

(1) Building a Supportive Relationship with Others (our clients must have people who they can turn to in their pain and who can listen without anxiety)

(2) Maintaining a Relaxed Body (our clients learn to self-regulate by softening their muscles)

(3) Telling Their Story (producing a narrative IS integration and relegates loss to the past, allowing us to remember with love)

Case Study

Healing From Traumatic Grief

• •

Maria lost her husband Carlos after 25 years of marriage. The death was sudden and traumatic and Maria, who had survived childhood sexual and psychological abuse from her father, was now suffering from traumatic grief, a severe form of bereavement which may be similar to post-traumatic stress disorder. After three years of therapy which focused on the loss of her husband, the childhood abuse she survived and her lifelong pursuit of perfectionism, she joined Toastmasters International to help improve her self-confidence when speaking in public. The assignment was a brief speech on an inspirational moment, and following are her inspirational words.

I spent this week searching for the PERFECT inspirational moment. There had to be something I could find that is different from anything they had heard before. I asked two close confidants for "inspiration". Both said "Say something about what you have accomplished and what you've learned." I'm not ready for THAT! There has to be something easier. So I kept searching. This is what perfectionists do. Perfectionism is an unattainable goal. Perfectionists look for the perfect response, the perfect word, the perfect sounding note, the perfect tequila or the perfect inspiration. They believe there is one perfect answer and the rest is a failure. The only option is Black or White when the palate is full of 50 shades of gray. It becomes very difficult to be successful when striving for perfection.

Brene Brown says "Perfectionism is a twenty-TON shield that we lug around thinking it will protect us when, in fact, it's the thing THAT'S really preventing us from taking flight. Understanding the difference between healthy striving and perfectionism is critical to laying down the shield and picking up your life. Research shows that perfectionism hampers success. In fact, it's often the path to depression, anxiety, addiction, and life paralysis." Really? Well, that explains quite a bit.

While perfectionism has been rampant in many aspects of my life, none are more apparent and important to me than music. Truthfully, there is nothing more imperfect than a live performance of music no matter how excellent a musician you are. I suffered way too many years trying to be a perfect musician. Ask me how the concert went, and I would tell you which notes I missed, or how many I missed, OR the solo I messed up because I was so nervous about it needing to be perfect. That was definitely me more than 3 years ago, and I was not enjoying music. I was either good or bad. If I missed notes, it wasn't good. It still creeps in when I'm not paying attention, but I've come a long way in 3 years.

Listen to these words written by Timothy Gallwey in the book "The Inner Game of Tennis: The Classic Guide to the Mental Side of Peak Performance." "When we plant a rose seed in the earth, we notice that it is small, but we do not criticize it as "rootless and stemless. We treat it as a seed, giving it the water and nourishment required of a seed. When it first shoots up out of the earth, we don't condemn it as immature and underdeveloped; nor do we criticize the buds for not being open when they appear. We stand in wonder at the process taking place and give the plant the care it needs at each stage of its development. The rose is a rose from the time it is a seed to the time it dies. Within it, at all times, it contains its whole potential. It seems to be constantly in the process of change; yet at each state, at each moment, it is perfectly all right as it is."

It's the journey, not necessarily the destination, we should be enjoying. Because I've gained the courage to jump into the journey, I've met some amazing people and done some amazing things. Courageously, I have found teachers who years ago I would never have approached. "Most people don't aim too high and miss, they aim too low and hit." This is a quote by Bob Moawad, author of the book, "Whatever it Takes." My first teacher in this journey was the first horn of the local Orchestra, a student of a couple of the best horn teachers in the U.S., graduate of the best school of music, now the 3rd horn for a major US Symphony Orchestra. I almost gave up playing horn when suddenly I couldn't play well because we had changed how I breathed while playing. What was initially coming out was far from perfect. I had to learn to trust the process and let go of those negative thoughts. And I moved forward.

My current teacher/mentor, Micah, has been a member of the world's most famous brass ensemble, has performed with the best North American orchestras, a professor at an internationally renowned School of Music, given a Ted Talk, founder of his own company and president of an International Music Association. After all, if I am going to learn how to be a better horn player and performer why would I aim low?

By the time I played my first horn notes for Micah, we already had a relationship of trust. I was nervous none the less. The chatter in my head was there. No matter what I learned so far...there it was. Will he figure out that I'm not perfect? However, he took the pressure off and asked me to just play any scale, at whatever tempo I wanted. More chatter in my head. Though I took a deep breath and told myself to TRUST. I played the easiest scale so not to add something else to the stress. At the end, he asked me, "How did it feel?" To this day, I believe my words summed it up best..." I PLAYED A SCALE FOR MICAH (fist pump)". For that moment it didn't matter if I played a C Major scale or a d# minor scale. It didn't matter if I played it at a tempo of 40 or a tempo of 144. I, honestly, didn't care if it was good or bad. It was solely about the moment, the experience. Not everyone gets to sit across from someone at the top of the field (a Horn God) and play. And yet, eventually perfectionism creeps in. Eventually he assigned me an etude, which I looked at and decided that there was no way I could play it. I spent days avoiding it because I knew that I couldn't play it, let alone perfectly. Then I realized what was happening, took the tools he had taught me, and sat down and started to learn it.

Did I ever play it perfectly...NO!

Did I play it better than I expected...HELL YES!

But it's the experiences I've had, the people I've met that make me the happiest. My world has become wide open. And strangely with letting go of perfectionism, I've become more confident. The journey is FAR from complete.

I've learned a few things along the way.
- *All of the time the audience is there to hear music. They most often don't hear the few mistakes that we know are there. Focus on the music, and they come away happy.*
- *In a 90-minute concert, I easily play more than 1000 notes. If I missed notes, I'm still a 90% player. Pretty good? Guess what? I don't miss 100 notes, I miss 20 or 25 or 50. Sometimes only 5. Not bad!! Keep perspective!*
- *Realization that the person(s) next to you and around you are mostly likely so concerned about their own notes/performance that they don't have time to sit in judgement of you.*
- *Every musician, no matter their level of excellence, misses notes and makes errors. Their "misses" may be different than yours, but to make your goal to be as perfect as one of the current greatest horn players would make them chuckle as they will tell you...they are not perfect. Strive for your own level of excellence.*

Horn playing is not much different than public speaking; similar struggle, words instead of notes.

Micah states that "Public speaking is a fantastic laboratory for studying how we choose to negatively change things when we're better served staying calm, cool and consistently you...authentic." And here we are, practicing, learning, experiencing the art of speaking to become better, but not perfect.

It's not easy to unlearn this habit of perfectionism, so part of the journey is to become aware when it has taken hold. Then to have the courage to go forth and just be imperfect, or more exact, just be your authentic imperfect self. Because at the end of the day, that's all any of us are.

Reprinted with Maria's permission

CHAPTER 9

The Next Phase For Trauma Treatment

. . . .

As our knowledge of the brain becomes more sophisticated, our ability to treat clients improves. Every year we have a clearer understanding of how neuroscience and psychotherapy interact to produce a more effective trauma treatment.

We also have a greater understanding of how relationships influence brain development and psychopathology especially in infancy and early childhood. And as we learn more about this relationship we also increase our understanding of the relationship between early attachment and the therapeutic relationship. These are key components in psychotherapy, including trauma therapy.

And, of course, the more we learn about brain dysregulation the closer we get to creating more effective interventions. The ability of clients to learn self-regulation is essential to treatment of traumatic stress.

Trauma therapists are incorporating research from alternative and complementary disciplines. They are beginning to use techniques such as Yoga, Tai Chi and dance to treat PTSD as well as massage and body manipulations to treat traumatic stress. They are looking at interventions from disciplines as diverse as Occupational Therapy, Physical Therapy, Speech and Language Therapy, and Chiropractic. Therapy dogs are used in hospitals, schools and correctional facilities because of the positive effect they have on healing. Techniques are also emerging from the expressive arts and music to help treat the traumatized brain.

Eric Gentry (2016) has developed a cutting-edge system he calls Forward Facing Trauma Therapy (FFTT) which attacks trauma and its destructive symptomology at its source, the dysregulation of our autonomic nervous systems and hypervigilant threat response caused by adaptation to painful past experiences. Dr. Gentry provides a step-by-step guide for implementing the three-pronged FFTT methodology and demonstrates how and why the techniques work so effectively. He also explains how anyone experiencing stress can apply FFTT to achieve immediate change and an enduring sense of joy, self-worth, and personal integrity. It is a three-phased treatment and self-empowerment protocol designed to: restore homeostasis, align our behavior with our values, and identify and manage our triggers. This is a system that draws on the latest research, and can be used by almost all therapists.

Restore homeostasis. We can't just flip a switch and reboot our brains into a state of harmony and homeostasis. But we can indirectly force the neurological systems responsible for the fight-or-flight response to loosen their grip by developing the skill of interoception, or "bodifulness," which allows us to become fluent in the silent yet eloquent language of our bodies. We won't be able to entirely prevent our bodies from producing the stress response (nor would we want to when confronted with a real threat to our safety), but we will be able to rein it in rapidly and effectively when it runs amok.

Align our behavior with our values. In the throes of the stress response, we're much more likely to lose control and behave in ways that are destructive to ourselves and others. Reducing the frequency and intensity of these episodes is certainly a worthwhile goal in itself. However, an equally important goal is learning to act in accordance with our ideals, values, and principles. Dr. Gentry shows how we can apply "intentionality" to achieve this goal through a process of self-exploration that culminates in the development of a written Covenant and Code of Honor. These documents - and the exercises that go with them - enable us to navigate the vicissitudes of life with intentionality and purpose.

Identify and manage our triggers. When we experience chronic stress, we can enter a state of hypervigilance in which our threat detection systems are always running on overdrive. In that state, anything we unconsciously associate with past painful learning experiences - a sound, smell, or physical sensation - can plunge us into a full-scale fight, flight or freeze response. As a result, we may be triggered dozens or even hundreds of times each day. The last phase of FFTT involves learning how to identify our triggers and negate their power by applying our new skills of self-regulation and intentionality on an ongoing basis in real-time.

Dr. Gentry (2016) observes that any meaningful approach to eliminating the scourge of chronic stress must satisfy a number of critical requirements. First and foremost, it should employ methods that anyone can learn to apply with a little practice and dedication. Buddhist monks spend decades mastering advanced meditation techniques that enable them to control their heart rate, suppress their involuntary startle responses, and "light up" different parts of their brains at will. However, few of us possess the time or discipline to devote ourselves in this way. Any realistic approach should reduce the impact of stress on our lives as quickly and efficiently as possible.

Dr. Gentry (2016) also reminds us that the stress response operates along a continuum. Some of us are contending with the relatively mild levels of arousal associated with such things as getting stuck in traffic when we're late for work. At the other end of the spectrum, some of us are trying to cope with the life-altering panics and intrusive thoughts that come with full-blown PTSD. A viable stress reduction approach should therefore work effectively for everyone, regardless of where they find themselves on the continuum.

This surely is an exciting time to be learning about trauma therapy.

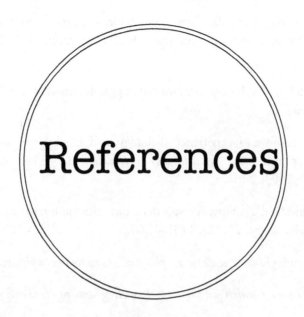

References

American Psychiatric Association. (1952). *Diagnostic and statistical manual of mental disorders* (1st ed.). Washington, DC: Author.

American Psychiatric Association. (1968). *Diagnostic and statistical manual of mental disorders* (2nd ed.). Washington, DC: Author.

American Psychiatric Association. (1980). *Diagnostic and statistical manual of mental disorders* (3rd ed.). Washington, DC: Author.

American Psychiatric Association. (1987). *Diagnostic and statistical manual of mental disorders* (3rd ed., text rev.). Washington, DC: Author.

American Psychiatric Association. (1994). *Diagnostic and statistical manual of mental disorders* (4th ed.). Washington, DC: Author.

American Psychiatric Association. (2000). *Diagnostic and statistical manual of mental disorders* (4th ed., Text Rev.). Washington, DC: Author.

American Psychiatric Association. (2013). *Diagnostic and statistical manual of mental disorders* (5th ed.). Washington, DC: Author.

Baranowsky, A.B., Gentry, J.E., & Schultz, D.F. (2005*). Trauma practice: Tools for stabilization & recovery*. New York: Huber & Hogrefe.

Barrett, D. (1996). Dreams in multiple personality disorder. In D. Barrett (Ed.), *Trauma and dreams* (pp. 68–81). Cambridge, MA: Harvard University Press.

Beard, G. (1878). Remarks upon jumpers or jumping Frenchmen. *The Journal of Nervous and Mental Diseases* 5: 526.

Benish, S., Imel, Z., & Wampold, B. (2007). The relative efficacy of bona fide psychotherapies for treating post-traumatic stress disorder: A meta-analysis of direct comparisons. *Clinical Psychology Review, 28* (7), 1281.

Bentley, S. (2005). *A short history of PTSD: From Thermopylae to Hue soldiers have always had a disturbing reaction to war.* Retrieved from http://www.vva.org/archive/TheVeteran/2005_03/feature_HistoryPTSD.htm

Bisson, J., & Andrew, M. (2005). Psychological treatment of post-traumatic stress disorder (PTSD). *Cochrane Database of Systematic Reviews, 18.*

Brunner, J. (2000). Will, desire and experience: Etiology and ideology in the German and Austrian medical discourse on war neuroses. *Transcultural Psychiatry, 37* (3), 295–320. doi:http://dx.doi.org/10.1177/136346150003700302

Callahan, R. (2001). Thought field Therapy: A response to our critics and scrutiny of some old ideas of social science. *Journal of Clinical Psychology,* 57 (10), 1251–1260.

Charcot, J. M. (1868). "Histologie de la sclérose en plaques". *Gazette des hopitaux, Paris, 41,* 554–55.

Cooper, Mick. (2008). *Essential research findings in counseling and psychotherapy:* The Facts are Friendly. London: Sage Publications.

Da Costa, J. (1871). On irritable heart; a clinical study of a form of functional cardiac disorder and its consequences. *The American Journal of the Medical Sciences* (61), 18–52.

Danieli, Yael. (2010). *International handbook of multigenerational legacies of trauma.* New York: Springer Publishing.

Department of Veterans Affairs. (2010) *VA/DoD clinical practice guidelines for management of post-traumatic stress.* Retrieved from http://www.healthquality.va.gov/PTSD-Full-2010c.pdf

Dubi, M., Raggi, M. & Reynolds, J. (2012). *Distance supervision: The PIDIB model. Vistas, Alexandria, VA: American Counseling Association.* Article 82.

Department of Veterans Affairs. (2012). *Report on VA specific Operation Enduring Freedom [OEF], Operation Iraqi Freedom [OIF], and Operation New Dawn [OND] veterans coded with potential PTSD-revised.* Retrieved from http://www.publichealth.va.gov/docs/epidemiology/ptsd-report-fy2012-qtr3.pdf

Duncan, B., Miller, S. Sparks, J., Claud, D., Reynolds, L., Brown, J, & Johnson, L. (2003). The Session Rating Scale: Preliminary psychometric properties of a "working" alliance measure. *Journal of Brief Therapy, (3)* 1, 3–12.

Foa, E., Hembree, E., & Rothbaum, B. (2007). *Prolonged exposure therapy for PTSD: Emotional processing of traumatic experiences, therapist guide.* New York: Oxford Press.

Frankl, V. E. (1967). Logotherapy and existentialism. *Psychotherapy: Theory, Research & Practice, 4* (3), 138–142. doi:http://dx.doi.org/10.1037/h0087982

Frankl, V. (1959). *Man's search for meaning.* Boston: Beacon Press.

Fussell, P. (1989). *Wartime: Understanding and behavior in the Second World War.* New York: Oxford University Press.

Gentry, J.E. (2016) *Forward facing trauma therapy: healing the moral wound.* Sarasota, FL: Compassion Unlimited.

Genty, J. E. (1998). *Trauma Recovery Scale*. Retrieved from http://psychink.com/ti2012/wp-content/upload s/2012/06/207TICAssign.20111.pdf

Gentry, J. E. (2002). Compassion fatigue: A crucible of transformation. *The Journal of Trauma Practice, 1* (3/4), 37–61.

Gentry, J. E. & Schmidt, I. M. (1998). Safety reconnaissance with survivors of trauma and traumatic death. In Figley. (Ed.), *Death and trauma II*. New York: Brunner-Mazel.

Hall, R. C. (2012). Compensation neurosis: A too quickly forgotten concept? *Journal of the American Academy of Psychiatry and the Law, 40*(3), 390–398. Retrieved from http://search.proquest.com/docview/128406436 6?accountid=34899

Hayes, S. C., Strosahl, K. D., and Wilson, K. G. (2012). *Acceptance and commitment therapy: The process and practice of mindful change* (2 ed.). New York: Guilford Press.

Herrmann, A. (2007). Heimweh, or homesickness. *The Yale Review, 95* (3), 23–32. doi: http://dx.doi. org/10.1111/j.1467-9736.2007.00306.x

Herman, J. (1992). *Trauma and Recovery*. New York: Basic Books.

Hofer, J. (1934). Medical dissertation on nostalgia. (C. K. Anspach, Trans.). *Bulletin of the History of Medicine, 2*, 376–391.

Janet, P. (1899). *De l'Automatisme Psychologique*.

Jones, E., Fear, N., & Wessely, S. (2007). Shell shock and mild traumatic brain injury: A historical review. *The American Journal of Psychiatry, 164* (11), 1641–1645. doi:http://dx.doi.org/10.1176/appi.ajp.2007.07071180

Kardiner, A. (1941). *The traumatic neuroses of war*. New York: Paul B. Hoeber Inc.

Katerelos, T., Belanger, C., Payette, M., El-Baalbaki, G., Marhcand, A, & Perreault, M. (2015). A fresh look at anxiety disorders. (2015). The role of expectations in treatment outcome and symptom development in anxiety disorders. In *A fresh look at anxiety disorders*, 243–267. Croatia: Intech.

Langens, T. A., & Schüler, J. (2007). Effects of written emotional expression: The role of positive expectancies. *Health Psychology, 26*(2), 174–182. doi:http://dx.doi.org/10.1037/0278-6133.26.2.174

Lewis, R. (1918). *The soldier's heart and the effort syndrome*. Toronto: London Shaw.

Lind, J. E. (1937). Traumatic neurasthenia, especially "railway spine". *Medical Record, 146*, 65-71.

Linehan, M., Schmidt, H., Dimeff, L., Craft, J., Kanter, J., & Comtois, K. (1999). Dialectical behavior therapy for patients with borderline personality disorder and drug dependence. *The American Journal on Addictions* 8, 279–292.

Lynch, M. (2015). Factors influencing psychotherapy outcomes. *Masters of Social Work Clinical Outcomes, 57*.

Management of Post-Traumatic Stress Working Group (2010). *VA/DoD clinical practice guideline: Management of post-traumatic stress guideline summary*. Washington, DC: Veterans Health Administration, Department of Defense.

Meichenbaum, D., & Cameron, R. (1989). Stress inoculation training. In Michenbaum & Cameron (eds.), *Stress Reduction and Prevention*. New York: Springer Publishing.

Miller, S. D., Hubble, M. A., Chow, D. L., & Seidel, J. A. (2013). The outcome of psychotherapy: Yesterday, today, and tomorrow. *Psychotherapy, 50*(1), 88–97. doi:http://dx.doi.org/10.1037/a0031097

The National Center for Cognitive Behavioral Therapy. (n.d.). *Key concepts of cognitive behavioral therapy.* Retrieved from http://www.nacbt.org/whatiscbt.htm

Peterson, C. (2009). Positive psychology. *Reclaiming Children and Youth, 18* (2), 3–7. Retrieved from http://search.proquest.com/docview/852771573?accountid=34899

Raggi, M., Dubi, M., & Reynolds, J. W. (2008). The use of a pantheoretical case note format as a clinical tool. *The New Jersey Journal of Professional Counseling, 60,* 5–11.

Resick, P. A., & Schnicke, M. K. (1993). *Cognitive processing therapy for rape victims: A treatment manual.* Newbury Park, CA: Sage.

Saraswathi, K. N. (2013). Logotherapy. *Nursing Journal of India, 104* (1), 37-38. Retrieved from http://search.proquest.com/docview/1536920138?accountid=34899

Shapiro, F. (1989). Eye movement desensitization procedure: A new treatment for post-traumatic stress disorder. *Journal of Behavior Therapy and Experimental Psychiatry*, 20, 211–217.

Shapiro, F. (1996). Eye movement desensitization and reprocessing (EMDR): Evaluation of controlled PTSD research. *Journal of Behavior Therapy and Experimental Psychiatry, 27* (3), 209–218.

Tinnin, L., & Gantt, L. (2013). *The instinctual trauma response and dual brain dynamics: A guide for trauma therapy.* West Virginia: Linda Gantt.

Uddin, M., Aiello, A., Wildman, D., Koenen, K., Pawalec, G., De Los Santos, R., Goldmann, E., & Galea, S. (2010). Epigenetic and immune function profiles associated with posttraumatic stress disorder. *Proceedings from the National Academy of Science, 107* (20), 9470–9475.

Van der Hart, O., & Brown, P. (1992). Abreaction reevaluated. *Dissociation 5* (3), 127–140.

Weathers, F. W., Blake, D. D., Schnurr, P. P., Kaloupek, D. G., Marx, B. P., & Keane, T. M. (2013). *The Clinician-Administered PTSD Scale for DSM-5 (CAPS-5).* Interview available from the National Center for PTSD at www.ptsd.va.gov.

Weathers, F. W., Litz, B. T., Keane, T. M., Palmieri, P. A., Marx, B. P., & Schnurr, P. P. (2013). *The PTSD Checklist for DSM-5 (PCL-5).* Scale available from the National Center for PTSD at www.ptsd.va.gov.

Wolpe, J. (1954). Reciprocal inhibition as the main basis of psychotherapeutic effects. *Archives of Neurology and Psychiatry,* 72 (2), 205–226.

Worden, W. (2008). *Grief counseling and grief therapy: A handbook for the mental health practitioner* (4th Edition). New York: Springer Publishing Company.

World Health Organization. (2007). *The World Health Organization report: A safer future.* Retrieved from http://www.who.int/whr/2007/whr07_en.pdf.

Wyeth Pharmaceuticals. (1945, September). Wyeth Pharmaceuticals advertisement. *Life Magazine.*

Trauma History

·······················

From Hysteria To
Evidence-Based Treatment

A HISTORY OF TRAUMATIC WAR-RELATED
SITUATIONS AND DIAGNOSTIC TITLES

Our understanding of trauma, traumatic stress reactions, and the *posttraumatic stress disorder* (PTSD) diagnosis has developed gradually over time. Often misunderstood or left undiagnosed in the past, a variety of sequentially occurring military and clinical situations in the early 20th Century resulted in our current body of knowledge and practices. To better understand how our modern conceptualization and diagnostic title of PTSD is utilized, we must understand what occurred to shape the history of the diagnosis.

The diagnostic term PTSD is relatively new, but the symptoms that we conceptualize as PTSD have been recognized in various cultures for hundreds of years. Swiss military physicians in the 17th century were among the first to identify and name the constellation of symptoms that are diagnosed as *acute combat reaction* or posttraumatic stress disorder. *Nostalgia* was the specific label given to Swiss soldiers in 1678 by Dr. Johannes Hofer for a condition characterized by melancholy, incessant thinking of home, disturbed sleep or insomnia, weakness, loss of appetite, anxiety, cardiac palpitations, stupor, and fever (Hofer, 1934).

German doctors diagnosed similar symptoms among their troops at about the same time. These doctors referred to the condition as *heimweh* (homesickness) (Herrmann, 2007). Obviously, it was strongly believed the symptoms came about from the soldiers longing to return home from the military. This was partly due to the fact that many soldiers were young and had never been far from their hometowns. Most had also never been involved in military combat. Roughly about the same time, Spanish physicians coined the term *estar roto* when treating soldiers, a term that translates to a "broken" spirit or heart (Bentley, 2005).

Later, internal medicine doctor Jacob Mendez Da Costa studied Civil War veterans in the United States and discovered that many of them suffered from chest-thumping (tachycardia), anxiety, shortness of breath and fatigue in response to exertion. He called this syndrome *soldier's heart* or *irritable heart* (Da Costa, 1871). The symptoms also came to be called *Da Costa syndrome*.

The term *shell shock* has been associated with PTSD symptoms since World War One (Jones, Fear, & Wessely, 2007). It was believed the impact of the shells produced a concussion that disrupted the physiology of the brain; thus the term shell shock came into fashion. WWI generated stress theories based on models of the mind, such as Freud's *war neurosis* (Brunner, 2000), which he postulated was brought about by the inner conflict between a soldier's *war ego* and his *peace ego*. However these theories never gained wide acceptance.

Another diagnosis at the time, which gained little currency, was *neurasthenia*, sometimes also called *hysteria*. These titles were Victorian-era descriptions for anyone who suffered from excessive neurosis or nervousness and included many symptoms that would now be considered signs of PTSD. George Beard published his definitive text on neurasthenia (Beard, 1878). The following segment from his work is particularly insightful:

"The mental troubles are many and marked; on the emotional side, there are sadness, weariness, and pessimism; repugnance to effort, abnormal irritability; defective control of temper, tendency to weep on slight provocation; timidity. On the intellectual side, lessened power of attention, defective memory and will power . . .."

It is important to note that eventually, it was not just those "weak" in character who were identified as the ones developing these symptoms. This is reflected in the subtle change in terminology that took place near the end of World War II when *combat neurosis* began to give way to the term *combat exhaustion*. Author Paul Fussell stated that combat exhaustion, as well as the term *battle fatigue* (Fussell, 1989), suggested "a little rest would be enough to restore to useful duty a soldier who would be more honestly designated as insane." While the name change showed movement away from psychopathology, it didn't fit with the military model of "predisposition plus stress equals collapse", which worked its way back into military medicine.

As a result of the rise in numbers of afflicted soldiers, army researchers studied combat exhaustion, or combat fatigue, during World War II and the Korean War. Army physicians decided that unit cohesion was a crucial factor in surviving this syndrome. Also, replacement soldiers were more prone to combat exhaustion because they were new to their units. The issue became so prevalent in society that treatments were offered in common newspapers and magazines. For example, there was an ad in the September 17, 1945 issue of Life Magazine (Wyeth Pharmaceuticals, 1945) touting Wyeth Pharmaceuticals' products in treating both colic and battle reaction and mental trauma.

We have discussed the diagnosis of PTSD and its antecedents in combat populations, but in the 19th century, as railroad travel became much more common, so did railroad accident and for the first time civilians began to be diagnosed with variants of what we would now term PTSD. Individuals who survived railway accidents were often left with physical damage such as broken bones and burns. Victims of railway accidents were also referred to as having *Railway Spine* (Lind, 1937) as if their spinal cords had suffered a concussion that caused them to be more nervous or traumatized afterwards. This correlation is likely due to the fact that individuals were bouncing up and down for long periods of time on hard wooden seats. At the time, the relationship between the spinal column and the brain was not well understood. During this time, psychologists began noticing frequent cases of traumatic reactions among survivors of those accidents. Psychologist CTJ Rigler coined the term *compensation neurosis* (Hall, 2012) to describe these cases. The term "compensation" referred to a new law allowing people to sue for compensation from emotional suffering. Rigler believed that people were more likely to report their traumatic symptoms, or possibly exaggerate them, if they were going to be compensated.

19TH CENTURY MEDICAL PROFESSIONALS
AND THEIR CONTRIBUTIONS TO TREATMENT

Jean Charcot was the "father of modern neurology" and an educator who trained with a variety of individuals, including Sigmund Freud. In the mid 1800's, he worked with patients who were experiencing what was diagnosed at the time as "hysteria", a condition with similarities to the modern diagnosis of PTSD (Charcot, 1868). The symptoms of hysteria were common throughout Europe during this period. Not only were solders frequently fighting battles, civilians were also impacted on a near daily basis by conflict within their vicinity. Charcot was one of the first practitioners to utilize hypnosis to treat patients.

Jacob Mendez Da Costa, previously mentioned for his development of the term *soldier's heart* was one of the first individuals to teach and train individuals how to specifically treat the consequences of war. He recognized that soldiers were not experiencing cardiac conditions, but rather psychological conditions.

Also, in the late 1800s, Pierre Janet, a student of Jean Charcot, was one of the first individuals to note a connection between events of a person's past life and present day trauma. Janet also coined the terms *dissociation* and *subconscious* (Janet, 1899). He studied the *magnetic passion* or *rapport* between the patient and the hypnotist and developed an early theory about transference. As a student of Charcot, Janet also utilized hypnosis to treat PTSD symptoms. Around the same time, Sigmund Freud and his mentor Joseph Breuer also studied and published about the relationship between traumatic life events and subsequent psychological problems.

TWENTIETH CENTURY CONTRIBUTIONS

In 1918, cardiologist Sir Thomas Lewis studied *soldier's heart.* He later wrote the monograph *The Soldier's Heart and the Effort Syndrome* (Lewis, 1918). In this work, Lewis further defined soldier's heart by chest pain, dizziness, fatigue, palpitations, cold and moist hands, and sighing respiration. He also noted the condition was mainly associated with soldiers in combat but also occurred in individuals experiencing unusual events. Additionally, he noted the pain mimicked angina pectoris but was more closely connected to anxiety states. Also, the pain occurred after, rather than during, exercise.

Additionally, Abram Kardiner described the initial PTSD diagnostic criteria in 1941 in his seminal work *the traumatic neuroses of war* (Kardiner, 1941) as the persistence of startle responses and irritability, proclivity to explosive outbursts of aggression, fixation on the traumatic event, constriction of one's general level of personality functioning, and atypical dream life. Kardiner performed psychoanalysis upon clients diagnosed with PTSD, but felt that it was an ineffective model for treatment. His work served as the basis for the *Diagnostic and Statistical Manual (APA)* diagnostic criteria.

THE PREVALENCE OF PTSD

PTSD is arguably one of the most researched diagnoses of the 21th century. Although most people who experience a traumatic event will not develop PTSD, it is one of the most common and recognizable mental disorders due to its unique combination of symptoms. As military campaigns have continued across the world, researchers, physicians, and mental health professionals have increased our understanding of the systemic nature of the disorder through our interactions with veterans and their families.

In 2012, researchers at the Department of Veterans Affairs published a report that 29% of veterans who were involved in operations Enduring Freedom and Iraqi Freedom experienced symptoms of PTSD (Department of Veterans Affairs, 2012). This is a significant statistic, as 20% of any population being affected is considered to be an epidemic. Also, PTSD rates were found to be higher among veterans, police, firefighters, and EMS personnel in comparison with the overall population. This statistic further evidenced the claim that individuals in high-conflict careers are more prone to PTSD. The highest rates of PTSD (33%–50%) were found to exist with survivors of rape, military combat & captivity, ethnically or politically motivated internment, and genocide. Individuals who experience these extreme situations are at significant risk for vicariously sharing their traumatization. *Vicarious traumatization* (sometimes called secondary traumatization or compassion fatigue) occurs when a responding therapist is traumatized by client stories and experiences, resulting in anxiety and a loss of coping skills. Other symptoms can include social withdrawal, aggression, somatic symptoms, sleep problems, and mood swings.

PTSD AS A CONTAGION

Some researchers have posited that PTSD can be transferred from one family member to another across generations. In 2010, Danielli, an Israeli psychologist, and other authors wrote about the intergenerational transmission of the symptoms of PTSD in *Multigenerational Legacies of Trauma* (Danieli, 2010), a collection of trauma - related research. The authors explored the psychiatric and cultural ramifications of wars and conflicts dating back to World War One. Among many findings, one author noted that the children of Vietnam veterans had "more severe problems" than individuals whose parents were not involved in conflict. Another author in the work noted the mechanisms of symptom transmission as silence, over-disclosure, identification, and reenactment. This pattern of transmission has been evidenced in a variety of cultures throughout history. For example, researchers in America have explored how PTSD in the Native American population has been transferred from generation to generation.

GENETIC CHANGES IN INDIVIDUALS
WHO EXPERIENCE TRAUMA

Can trauma produce genetic changes in offspring? Research into the *Dutch Hunger Winter* of 1944 has resulted in significant findings, correlating trauma with epigenetic changes. Between 1944 and 1945, German forces isolated the Netherlands. As a result of blockades, Dutch individuals did not have access to necessary amounts of food. It has been speculated that individuals met only 30% of their daily caloric intake. Over 20,000 people died from malnutrition in that one year alone. Women who were pregnant were not able to receive the nutritional requirements necessary for a healthy pregnancy.

Researchers later studied the descendents of Dutch individuals who survived the winter. It was expected that some immediate descendents would be born smaller than average, which was found. It was also found that those children were more prone to psychosis, depression, and metabolic issues such as obesity and diabetes. Surprisingly, for 40 years or more, descendents continued to be born smaller than average, regardless of access to food. Further, researchers determined that descendents of malnourished mothers had greater incidences of health problems and mental health symptoms than national averages.

In 2010, the National Academy of Science released the results of a study on PTSD (Uddin, et al. 2010). The authors found that individuals with PTSD are often genetically different than people who do not have PTSD. In particular, individuals with PTSD have differences in immune system genes and brain cell growth. The results indicate that PTSD can physically change brain tissue through changes to an individual's genetic code. If this is true, PTSD can be transmitted from generation to generation by DNA. This is especially concerning considering the increasing rates of PTSD diagnoses.